REASONS
IV

REASONS
IV

Explaining the Reformed Perspective

Roger Van Harn

Illustrations: Paul Stoub
Cover: Dean Heetderks

Bible Way

Grand Rapids, Michigan

Library of Congress Cataloging in Publication Data

Van Harn, Roger, 1932–
   Reasons IV, explaining the Reformed perspective

   Bibliography: p.
   1. Theology, Reformed Church.
   I. Title. II. Title: Explaining the Reformed perspective.
BX9422.2.V27   230'.5   81-38457
ISBN 0-933140-29-0   AACR2

Always be prepared to give an answer to everyone who asks you to give the reason for the hope that you have. But do this with gentleness and respect. . . .

1 Peter 3:15–16 (NIV)

Contents

Preface

This is the last in a series of four books in the course entitled Reasons. *That title is borrowed from Peter's injunction to "Always be prepared . . . to give the reason for the hope that you have." It's a course that's intended, in the first three books, to help Reformed Christians give reasons for their faith when conversing with people of other faiths and, in this last book, to help them give reasons for their own perspective on the Christian faith when conversing with Christians of other traditions.*

Reasons *is offered as part of the* BIBLE WAY *curriculum for young adults. That doesn't mean this book and course won't be profitable for you if you don't think of yourself as falling into that rather vague category,* young adult. Reasons *can be used by a variety of age groups, from mature high school seniors to the oldest adults. All Christians of all ages should learn to give reasons for what they believe.*

Still it's particularly young adults who encounter and are seriously challenged by other faiths and other Christian ways of looking at life, the world, the church, and God's salvation. The late teens and early twenties are often unsettled years when young men and women are leaving their home communities and finding their own niche in life. The exposure to divergent views challenges them to explain what they believe and why they believe it. For the first time many are forced to give reasons for their own faith—not just traditional arguments but explanations intelligible to non-Christians or to Christians with different perceptions of Christ's teaching.

This book presents eight challenges to the Reformed perspective. From various other positions on the Christian spectrum, from "liberal" to "fundamentalistic," it presents questions that require answers. These are intended to prepare you, as a Reformed Christian, to understand the issues raised and respond to them in ways that reflect your own faith.

The author of this book and of the responses which will be handed out in class is Dr. Roger Van Harn. A graduate of Calvin College and Seminary (Grand Rapids, Michigan) and of Trinity Lutheran Seminary (Columbus, Ohio), Rev. Van Harn is at present pastor of the Grace Christian Reformed Church in Grand Rapids, Michigan. He is also the author of Searchlight *(Christian Reformed Board of Publications, 1968) and a number of articles in the* Reformed Journal *and* The Banner.

The session guides following each challenge have been prepared by the Education Department staff.

Harvey A. Smit
Director of Education

EXPLAINING WHY WE'RE REFORMED

Reasons is a course in apologetics, a field of theological study intended to equip Christians to make apology. Making apology doesn't mean saying "I'm sorry" or "apologizing" for Jesus. It means explaining our faith in ways that make sense to people who don't share our beliefs. To use biblical language, it means "to make a defense to any one who calls [us] to account for the hope that is in [us]. . ." (1 Pet. 3:15, RSV).

The first three books in the *Reasons* series dialogue with people who are not Christians or people who, while claiming to be Christian, seem to have diverged fundamentally from the Christian faith. There is a clear and distinct we-they dichotomy in *Reasons I, II,* and *III.* The challenges come from sects, cults, or modern world and life views. In each case the faith defended is Christian, in the broadest sense.

Reasons IV is different. The challenges come not from outside or from the fringes, but from within the circle of the Christian faith. They come from brothers and sisters in Christ who find our Reformed views suspect, unbiblical, or dangerously weak in some areas: dispensationalists, with quite different ideas of how God works in various periods of history; Lutherans, with contrasting concepts of the kingdom; evangelicals, to whom salvation without a conversion experience is inconceivable—these are the people who speak in the challenges of this book. They require of us a reasoned response. What we defend is not the Christian faith but the perspective on it commonly held in Reformed and Presbyterian churches.

This book is intended to help you interact sensitively with Christians of other theologies and traditions. It tries to teach a better comprehension of why these fellow believers interpret the Bible, express the faith, and hold the hope as they do. Why do some evangelicals astringently assert that anyone who says the Bible contains a single "mistake" has no Bible? Why do some adventists long for the rapture exclusively? Why do some followers of Jesus Christ speak of him as the "superstar"? Under such ideas lie some basic perspectives on the Christian faith that should be carefully reviewed. We owe fellow Christians the courtesy of listening humbly to their opinions and weighing carefully their criticisms.

But this book (and this course) is also intended to help you prepare to reply to such opinions and answer such criticisms. We, as Reformed Christians, should be ready to explain why we believe, act, think, worship, work, and live as we do. We should be able to give reasons for our own ways.

So if a friend asks how we can possibly baptize babies when the Bible clearly teaches that only believers should be baptized, or if an acquaintance inquires why we're looking for a Reformed or Presbyterian church (or any church at all) on a gorgeous vacation Sunday when we have the whole of God's creation to worship in, or if a neighbor asks how we as Christians could possibly approve government ownership of a bus line— we should be ready to give an answer. We owe an explanation both to ourselves and to our neighbors. It's to our own benefit as well as theirs to put the reasons for our faith into words.

This book presents eight challenges. Each raises one central question and offers several answers from varied Christian perspectives. The Reformed answer is one of those several.

We're asking you, together with others who are taking this course, to consider each challenge and determine how you might best respond. A group discussion should help you recognize the strengths and weaknesses of the Reformed position, how prepared or unprepared you are to explain that stand, and what your best response might be. A session guide following each challenge offers suggestions to direct your discussion.

After the group discussion (or sometime during it) we've suggested that your teacher or discussion leader hand out the author's response to the challenge. The approach the author takes is not the one, authoritative answer—the only Reformed way to respond. You may disagree with it. You may have already reached some other conclusion. Still each response will give you, for future reference, the thoughtful ideas of someone who has studied this question with care and reflected deeply upon it from the Reformed perspective. An envelope has been provided on the back cover of this book for storing the author's responses.

It's our earnest hope that this course will not only strengthen your understanding of your own faith, but also begin to equip you to deal confidently and positively with people who hold very different views. It's with that hope that we offer this book for your study.

Harvey A. Smit
Director of Education

CHALLENGE 1

WHO IS JESUS?

Once there was a boy who heard
the preacher say God and Jesus a lot.
His father said God
when he was mad.
His mother said Jesus
when he got dirt
on the carpet.
Now he is old enough
to say Jesus and God.
He can say Jesus
without even thinking.
He can say God
and not even mean it.

Herbert Brokering, *I—Opener,* p. 14

A street-corner evangelist was swinging a Bible and shouting, "Jesus is the powerhouse! Are you plugged in? Jesus is the transformer! Are you wired up? Jesus is the cable carrying that current from God Almighty! Is your trolley on? Oh, is your trolley on?"

The speaker must have detected the animation in my face, alone in the small group of sullen listeners who surrounded him, and mistaken it for approval. He therefore turned on the box on which he was standing and said to me:

"Brother, have you found Christ?"
  "Is he lost again?" I said.

Peter De Vries, The Mackerel Plaza, p. 141

I don't know how to love him
What to do how to move him
I've been changed, yes really changed
In these past few days when I've seen myself
I seem like someone else.

I don't know how to take this
I don't see why he moves me
He's a man, he's just a man
And I've had so many men before
In very many ways
He's just one more.

Mary Magdalene in Jesus Christ Superstar*

Where are you from, Jesus? What do you want, Jesus?
Tell me.
You've got to be careful—you could be dead soon—could well be.
Why do you not speak when I have your life in my hands?
How can you stay quiet? I don't believe you understand.

Pilate in Jesus Christ Superstar*

Jesus Christ, Jesus Christ
Who are you? What have you sacrificed?
Jesus Christ Superstar
Do you think you're what they say you are?

Chorus in Jesus Christ Superstar*

A man who was merely a man and said the sort of things Jesus said would not be a great moral teacher. He would either be a lunatic—on a level with the man who says he is a poached egg—or else he would be the Devil of Hell. You must make your choice. Either this man was, and is, the Son of God: or else a madman or something worse. You can shut Him up for a fool, you can spit at Him and kill Him as a demon, or you can fall at his feet and call Him Lord and God.

C. S. Lewis, Mere Christianity, p. 42

Marty Brunner was 6'2" and weighed 222 pounds. Everyone recognized him from the newspapers. Some had even seen him on TV. Marty played center for State on the championship team that won the conference but lost the bowl game. During the off-season he visited youth groups around the state. He was, as the newspapers said, "first a Christian and second a football player."

Brunner's public appearances always followed the same pattern. Walking to the front of a crowded auditorium, Marty carried a Bible and a football. Before saying anything, he looked around for a place to lay the ball. Usually he left it on a table in the corner or on a vacant seat. Then he returned to the lectern, opened his Bible, and began to speak.

I'm sure all of you have questions about what went wrong in the big game. That's the first thing people ask me. I've heard fifty-six opinions about what went wrong. And I'm here to say that just one thing went wrong: we lost! I'll be glad to answer questions about the game later, but I'll have no excuses. We lost, and we can't replay it. We can just look at next season—and if anyone has any doubts, we'll be back to win.

(applause)

But the most important question is not, "Why did we lose the game?" The most important question is, "Who is Jesus?" And today I want to share with you who Jesus is to me.

When we set up for a play on the field, everyone depends on the quarterback. They call me the "center," but I'm only the center of the line. The play and the players center on the quarterback. He must know the plays, read the defense, and call the signals for all of us. What he calls, we do.

In the game of life, Jesus is my quarterback. And on his team there are no losers. . . .

From Scripture and experience, Marty talked about his Christian faith and life. The game supplied more than enough illustrations. The equipment, the goal, the huddle, the coach, the trainers, the Gatorade, the game plan—all these helped him say what it meant for him to be a Christian. Marty made it clear that being a star football player was not what life was about. Following Jesus was all that mattered.

But who is Jesus? Like Marty Brunner many people have struggled with that question and come up with their own personal answers. Hyam Maccoby, a Jewish teacher, studied the Scriptures to uncover the identity of Jesus. In 1973 he published the conclusion to his search:

> Jesus was a good man who fell among Gentiles. That is to say, he fell among those who did not understand that to turn him into a god was to diminish him. He tried to bring about the kingdom of God on earth, and he failed; but the meaning of his life is in the attempt, not in the failure. As a Jew, he fought not against some metaphysical evil but against Rome. Yet the movement which denied his life by deifying him misrepresented him as being opposed to the people whom he most loved and on whose behalf he fought.
>
> Hyam Maccoby, *Revolution in Judea*, p. 255

Is that who Jesus really is—or was Bruce Barton right? After suffering through years of Sunday school classes, Barton had given up hope of even liking Jesus. But for some reason becoming a businessman changed his attitude. Wiping his mind clear of all books, sermons, and Sunday school lessons, Barton began reading the Bible again. Noting the collapse of John the Baptist's movement, he was impressed by Jesus' success:

> He started with much less reputation than John and a much smaller group of followers. He had only twelve, and they were untrained simple men, with elementary weaknesses and passions. Yet because of the fire of his personal conviction, because of his marvelous instinct for discovering their latent powers, and because of his unwavering faith and patience, he molded them into an organization which carried on victoriously.
>
> Bruce Barton, *The Man Nobody Knows*, p. 30

"Wist ye not that I must be about my father's *business*?" he said. He thought of his life as *business*. What did he mean by business? To what extent are the principles by which he conducted his business applicable to ours? And if he were among us again, in our highly competitive world,

would his business philosophy work?

Bruce Barton, *The Man
Nobody Knows,* p. 162

Eleven years before Bruce Barton discovered that the "real" Jesus was a business executive, Bouck White saw Jesus as a social revolutionary on behalf of those oppressed by the industrial age:

> The carpenter of Nazareth is the democracy's chief asset; to suffer themselves to be defrauded of their birthright in him, was criminal negligence. He is the greatest arouser of the masses which human annals have recorded. "He stirreth up the people," is his biography in five words.... His footprints through Palestine were dragons' teeth, raising up a harvest of armed souls, helmeted for warrior work. Gifted with vision into the world of the unseen, he enlisted all the powers of that unseen world on the side of the disinherited. His theology had an inflammatory purpose. His ethics was the ethics of self-respect, a brand of ethics which is the destroyer of servitude and the begetter of freedom in every age and under every sky.

Bouck White, *The Call of
the Carpenter,* pp. 305, 306

Was White right? Who *is* Jesus?

Albert Schweitzer traced the history of attempts to discover who the "real" Jesus was. He concluded that Jesus expected the kingdom of God to be fully established on earth by his own ministry and death. The fact that Jesus was mistaken does not make him less important to us:

> He comes to us as One unknown, without a name, as of old, by the lakeside, He came to those men who knew Him not. He speaks to us the same word: "Follow thou me!" and sets us to the tasks which He has to fulfill for our time. He commands. And to those who obey Him, whether they be wise or simple, He will reveal Himself in the toils, the conflicts, the sufferings which they shall pass through in his fellowship, and, as an ineffable mystery, they shall learn in their own experience Who He is.

Albert Schweitzer, *The Quest of
the Historical Jesus,* p. 401

The question "Who is Jesus?" is not a new one; it has plagued two thousand years of church history. The Gospel writers wrestled with that question, each answering it in his own way. In fact no person who appears in the pages of those Gospels could escape answering. "He is beside himself," said members of his family (Mark 3:21). "He has a demon," said the Pharisees (Mark 3:22). On it went—first the question, then the answers. The early church struggled with the question, split over the question, and convened councils to answer the question. But the question never died, and the answers never seemed to explain him fully. And what a variety of answers! Are they all talking about the same person?

Who *is* Jesus? The answers given in this chapter have something in common. Each person answered out of his experience with life and the world. Each answer made Jesus fit what someone knew or believed was true.

Marty played football. He tried to say who Jesus was by using illustrations from the game.

Hyam Maccoby is a Jewish scholar. He

knows about Jewish faith, life, and history. He read the New Testament and said who Jesus was in terms of the Jewish problem with the Roman Empire.

Bruce Barton was a businessman. Business gave him a new way of reading the Gospels and of attempting to say who Jesus was.

Bouck White was a leader who cared about democracy and freedom for the oppressed people. He saw Jesus as a social revolutionary who championed the cause of the poor.

Albert Schweitzer was a theologian and a medical doctor. He saw suffering in the world and knew the compassion of Jesus. These both played their parts in his belief that Jesus was a mistaken hero who is worthy to be followed even today.

The Pharisees said Jesus was the prince of demons because he cast out demons. His family said he was out of his mind because of the dangers to which he exposed himself. From the days of the New Testament to the present day both his friends and foes have said who Jesus is in ways that made him fit their experience and understanding.

Who *is* Jesus? Is there one right answer? And may we (must we) say who Jesus is in ways that make him fit our personal experience and understanding?

FOR FURTHER READING

Bonhoeffer, Dietrich. *Christology.* New York: Harper & Row Publishers, Inc., 1966.

> The famous Lutheran thinker gives a brief theological address to the question, "Who art thou, Lord?"

Lewis, C. S. *Mere Christianity.* London: Geoffrey Bles, 1952.

> Book IV of this volume, "Beyond Personality: or First Steps in the Doctrine of the Trinity," is a clear, easily read, easily understood presentation of how we should see Jesus Christ and what that means for us as Christians.

Muggeridge, Malcolm. *The End of Christendom.* Grand Rapids, Mich.: Wm. B. Eerdmans Pub. Co., 1980.

> The second part of this small book, "But not of Christ," presents an understanding of the incarnate presence of Christ in our world as absolute love and our only hope for the future.

SESSION GUIDE

CHALLENGE 1   WHO IS JESUS?

A. Personal notes/questions on Challenge 1

B. Group activity

   With others in your group, reach an agreement on what is the single most important answer you can give to the question "Who is Jesus?" Write your answer in the space below, limiting it to one very short sentence. Try to find at least one scriptural reference that supports your statement.

   Jesus is. . . .

C. For class discussion

   1. How do you know your answer to section *B* is valid? In other words, what is a "good" confession about Jesus?

   2. Apply your criteria (from answer 1 above) to the statements about Jesus found in Challenge 1. Do any of these statements fail to meet your standards? Explain.

3. In what ways is it good to fit Jesus to our experiences? In what ways can it be dangerous?

4. Look back at your own summary (from section *B*) of who Jesus is. Compare it with Response 1.

D. For reference

Q & A 1 of the Heidelberg Catechism:

What is your only comfort
in life and in death?

That I am not my own,
but belong—
   body and soul,
   in life and in death—
to my faithful Savior Jesus Christ.

   He has fully paid for all my sins with his precious blood,
   and has set me free from the tyranny of the devil.
   He also watches over me in such a way
   that not a hair can fall from my head
   without the will of my Father in heaven:
   in fact, all things must work together for my salvation.

Because I belong to him,
Christ, by his Holy Spirit,
assures me of eternal life
and makes me whole-heartedly willing and ready
from now on to live for him.

See also the Westminster Shorter Catechism, Q & A 21 and following.

WHICH CHURCH?

Once there was a church
that couldn't agree.
They always kept saying
the majority rules.
So they installed a computer.
Every member can dial in
and get opinions
on anything programed in.
The computer is very busy
keeping the opinions correct.
The people never vote anymore
or have congregational meetings....
They just dial in
and get the majority opinion.
No one sees any reason
for meeting anymore.
The majority is voting to stay away.
They feel as long as they know
the majority opinion
everything is going fine.

Herbert Brokering, *I—Opener*, p. 42

The Friendliest Church in Town
A Going Church for a Coming Christ
Clear-headed, Warm-hearted, Willing-handed
The Church that Cares about You
Independent, Bible-Centered
Bring a copy of this ad and receive a free copy of the pastor's book

—Notes from church ads in a Saturday newspaper

Frank S. Mead, *Handbook of Denominations in the United States,* Table of Contents

Born into a strong evangelical Protestant family (Dutch Reformed), I became a Roman Catholic while studying philosophy at Yale. I did so for the only valid and honest reason anyone ever should become a Catholic, or a Protestant, or a Christian, or an atheist: because I believe it is true.

But I also believe everything affirmed and emphasized by evangelical Protestantism is true.

Peter Kreeft, "Toward Uniting the Church," *The Reformed Journal,*
January 1979, p. 10–14

They were an unlikely match. Whatever similarities existed between them were known only to the computer and now belong to the mysteries of the electronic age. Fortunately, dormitory life and Midwestern State University did not require that roommates be friends. At first their paths crossed so infrequently that if their sleeping hours had not overlapped, they could have doubted each other's existence. It was not until the fifth week of the first quarter that Tom saw Dennis in broad daylight at the cafeteria. With a touch of humor that barely disguised his embarrassment, he asked, "Aren't we roommates?"

They talked over lunch—mostly about the food. Each tried to recall the details of the profile the university had sent to introduce the other. The effort to make them brothers by mail had failed. They lightly sketched their families with pretended detachment, being careful to hide more than they disclosed. Finding that they both hated the food and disliked their classes, the distance between them was at least bridged.

That weekend Tom didn't go home to his family farm in Jackson County. Dennis was already accustomed to staying around since the remnant of his family lived in Paterson, New Jersey. At 4:30 on Saturday afternoon Tom walked into the room with a newspaper under his arm. With no schedules to excuse themselves, they were again face to face.

"Checking the news?"

"No," said Tom.

"Sports?"

"No."

"Then you must be checking out what's happening tonight," said Dennis, as though it would be his last guess.

Without looking up, Tom said, "No. I'm looking for a church to go to tomorrow morning."

Silence fell. Tom spread the newspaper on the desk and found the church ads. Box announcements sprinkled with an assortment of emblems were spread across two pages, resembling a view of the Midwest flatlands from ten thousand feet. In the center the smiling faces of a young white mother and father with one son and one daughter accompanied the direct command: "Attend the Church of Your Choice." Dennis read over Tom's shoulder.

"Holy cow!"

For a moment, at least, they were getting together.

Which church should Tom choose and why?

Before rushing to answer, consider the history behind the question. Tom's question is a fairly new one.

For the first 300 years after Christ, no one would have asked, "Which church should Tom choose and why?" During those cen-

turies the choice was between Christ and Caesar. Even when the persecutions were lifted, the choice was between serving Christ or obeying the Roman Empire. Whether Christians lived before, during, or after a particular wave of persecution, the line was drawn by Roman policy: Caesar first, and after that comes any loyalty you please. For Christians, Jesus Christ was Lord. He could be second to none. Their faith was seen as a threat to the imperial security. So for the first three centuries after Christ, Tom's question would not have been asked or understood.

The next fourteen centuries were different. Troubles abounded for the church, but they were troubles of a different sort. For most Christians there was one church. The few who had the choice of another church did so under a new threat, this time from the established church. Even after the Protestant Reformation, few Christians enjoyed the freedom of personally choosing one church over another. In fact, it was not until the beginning of the eighteenth century that Tom's question could be widely understood. That means Tom's question has been

asked and understood for less than three hundred years. Christians who live in Canada and the United States, and who are accustomed to church directories in motels and church ads in newspapers, should catch the history lesson behind Tom's question. His question is *new*.

Tom kept looking at the ads. Dennis watched over his shoulder. Which church should he choose and why? The history lesson behind the question was not as important as the problem it raised. Tom was a Christian. He had been taught well in his home and church. Back home his rural church was named "Evangelical and Reformed," "E and R" for short. Its roots lay in the German Reformation, and it was the product of one merger and a leftover from another. They learned the Heidelberg Catechism Q & A 54:

What do you believe concerning the "holy catholic church"?

I believe that the Son of God,
   through his Spirit and Word,
   out of the entire human race,
   from the beginning of the world to its
      end,
gathers, protects, and preserves for himself
   a community chosen for eternal life
      and united in true faith.
And of this community I am and always
   will be a living member.

Back home it had not been difficult to believe that the church was "chosen and united" in Christ. But now he was in his ninth-floor dormitory room in a large city looking at a page of church ads. Christ chose one church from the entire human race, he had learned. Now he must choose one church for one Sunday morning from among a multitude of churches.

What were his choices? The city directory listed 783 churches, the yellow pages 628, and the newspaper ads 189. "At least that narrows the field," he thought. Here and there he saw words like "Reformed" and "Evangelical," but none of them looked like "E and R." The three headings didn't help. PROTESTANT, CATHOLIC, JEWISH, they read. ORTHODOX stood at the bottom by itself as though it didn't know where it belonged. The lists in fine print undereach unbalanced and seemed to have no connection with the boxes. It was too much. His decision to attend worship seemed right, and buying the newspaper seemed responsible, but choosing a church in this city was not a matter for the innocent.

Tom walked to the window. He felt alone even though Dennis was there. Across the street he saw a large church building with a tower and sign: University Baptist Church.

"You should have been here last weekend," Dennis said. "I talked about religion with our suitemates in their room."

"Do they know where they're going?" asked Tom.

"Jim knows where he's *not* going. He's an atheist. The only time he went to church was when his parents got divorced. He rebelled for awhile and went to church against their wishes, but he didn't stay. Al has been going to a small group that's into studying the Bible and ecology. I don't think they have a place and I'm not sure of the name."

Tom was relieved that Dennis talked so freely. "Do you have a church?" he asked.

"I'm not in a hurry to get involved here. When I do it will be at the Newman [Catholic] Center. Before I came here, I worked with Backup—that's really B.C.C.O.P.—and it stands for the Black Catholic Caucus of Paterson. I got burned out and want a break. I'll go to mass when I need it, but the books come first."

Tom stood quietly looking out the window. The sign across the street had answered his question for tomorrow morning. He would attend the University Baptist Church. Why? Because it was there.

But that was not the end of his question. There were more Sundays and more quarters at Midwestern State. Tom believed what he had learned: *Of this community I am and always will be a living member.* But what did that mean for where he was now?

FOR FURTHER READING

Dulles, Avery. *Models of the Church.* Garden City, N.Y.: Doubleday & Co., 1974.

A comprehensive study by a Roman Catholic theologian of various Christian understandings of the church.

Osterhaven, M. Eugene. *The Spirit of the Reformed Tradition.* Grand Rapids, Mich.: Wm. B. Eerdmans Pub. Co., 1971.

The second section of this excellent book concentrates on the Reformed church as a church always reforming itself and doing so according to the Word of God.

SESSION GUIDE

CHALLENGE 2   WHICH CHURCH?

A. Personal notes/questions on Challenge 2

B. Questions for discussion

1. Why should Tom attend church? Why not be a private Christian and settle for reading the Bible and/or watching TV church? Why church?

2. What basic things should Tom consider when looking for a church home? That is, what standards can Tom apply to narrow his choices to churches that are *true* churches? Compare your answers to Article 29 of the Belgic Confession. *Some basic things Tom should consider in looking for a church home would be like it says in article 29 of the Belgic Confession one that the pure doctrine of the gospel is preached and that all things are managed according to the pure word of God.*

3. Once Tom has narrowed his choices to a certain number of true churches, he will need additional, practical guidelines to make his final, single selection. If you were in Tom's position, which of the following pieces of advice would you regard as important? (Mark with a 1.) As unimportant? (Mark with a 3.) As possibly useful, but not crucial? (Mark with a 2.)

   _3_ a. Choose a church from my own denomination.

   _3_ b. Choose a church most like the one I attended at home—in its membership, liturgy, programs.

   _1_ c. Choose a church that's warm and friendly and has a special ministry to students.

   _2_ d. Choose a church that's located nearby.

   _3_ e. Choose the church most of my friends choose.

   _1_ f. Choose a church with a preacher whose sermons stimulate and challenge me.

   _3_ g. Choose a church with a strong evangelism program.

   _2_ h. Choose a church that works hard for the alleviation of hunger and poverty.

   _3_ i. Choose a church that offers me some way to get directly involved in its ministry so I can be of genuine service.

   _2_ j. Choose a church that holds similar creeds and confessions to those of my denomination.

   ___ k. Other?

C. For reference

Q & A 54 of the Heidelberg Catechism:

What do you believe
concerning the "holy catholic church"?

I believe that the Son of God,
   through his Spirit and Word,
   out of the entire human race,
   from the beginning of the world to its end,
gathers, protects, and preserves for himself
   a community chosen for eternal life
     and united in true faith.
And of this community I am and always will be
   a living member.

Article XXVIII of the Belgic Confession:

We believe, since this holy congregation is an assembly of those who are saved, and outside of it there is no salvation, that no person of whatsoever state or condition he may be, ought to withdraw from it, content to be by himself; but that all men are in duty bound to join and unite themselves with it; maintaining the unity of the Church; submitting themselves to the doctrine and discipline thereof; bowing their necks under the yoke of Jesus Christ; and as mutual members of the same body, serving to the edification of the brethren, according to the talents God has given them.

And that this may be the more effectually observed, it is the duty of all believers, according to the Word of God, to separate themselves from all those who do not belong to the Church, and to join themselves to this congregation, wheresoever God has established it, even though the magistrates and edicts of princes were against it, yea, though they should suffer death or any other corporal punishment. Therefore all those who separate themselves from the same or do not join themselves to it act contrary to the ordinance of God.

Excerpt from Article XXIX of the Belgic Confession:

The marks by which the true Church is known are these: If the pure doctrine of the gospel is preached therein; if it maintains the pure administration of the sacraments as instituted by Christ; if church discipline is exercised in punishing of sin; in short, if all things are managed according to the pure Word of God, all things contrary thereto rejected, and Jesus Christ acknowledged as the only Head of the Church. Hereby the true Church may certainly be known, from which no man has a right to separate himself.

Excerpt from Chapter 25 of the Westminster Confession of Faith:

II. The visible church . . . consists of all those throughout the world that profess the true religion; and of their children; and is the kingdom of the Lord Jesus Christ, the house and family of God, out of which there is no ordinary possibility of salvation.

CHALLENGE 3

WHAT'S AHEAD?

Although the earth's inner core may have been churning since 1936, not until 1958 were there to be signs of drastic changes. One of the first Cayce prophecies, pointing up this period, came in January 1934 and embraced several continents:

"As to the changes physical again: The earth will be broken up in the western portion of America.

"The greater portion of Japan must go into the sea.

"The upper portion of Europe will be changed as in the twinkling of an eye.

"Land will appear off the east coast of America."

Jess Stearn, *Edgar Cayce—The Sleeping Prophet,* p. 37

DANGER: IN CASE OF RAPTURE, GRAB THIS WHEEL

Bumper Sticker

Kurtz: Now what do you think is the next major problem facing the world?
Kahn: If the first problem is nuclear war and the second is the problem of accelerated growth, the next problem is the lack of a sense of meaning and purpose.

Paul Kurtz and Herman Kahn, *Images of the Future,* p. 108

If we do not learn from history, we shall be compelled to relive it. True. But if we do not change the future, we shall be compelled to endure it. And that could be worse.

Alvin Toffler, ed., *The Futurists,* p. 3

Do not look back. And do not dream about the future, either. It will neither give you back the past, nor satisfy your other daydreams. Your duty, your reward—your destiny—are *here* and *now.*

Dag Hammarskjold, *Markings,* p. 157

Good afternoon! It's 1:32 on the Golden Sound of radio, WNOW, and I'm Jane Bellamy, here—if I may—for another "Listen-In." Topics of the day are chosen from your requests, so if you want us to "Listen-In" on a favorite subject, just drop a postcard with your name, address, and suggestion to: "Listen-In," WNOW, Post Office Box 666.

The topic for today is "The Future," and it's timed right for our news director, Jack Jacobs. Studio sources say it's Jack's birthday tomorrow. What's the magic number, Jack?

(muffled groans mingled with laughs)
It looks like we may have lost another news director! He left here like there *is* no tomorrow! But "Jack will be back," as we say around town, and you'll hear him on Golden Sound news at 6.

Meanwhile our lines are open for "Listen-In." Our number is 633-3336. If you have an opinion, comment, or question about "The Future," we're "Listen-In." If the lines are busy, try again; we'll be taking a full hour of the future to talk about "The Future"! So keep dialing 633-3336.

(ring)

Jane: Hello, you're on "Listen-In."
Caller: Yes, hello, can you hear me, Jane?
Jane: Yes, we hear you. Go ahead. What do you have on the future?
Caller: I think it's stupid.
Jane: The future is stupid? What does...
Caller: No, not the future, but the topic. The *topic* is stupid. All you do is get people worried and upset. I used to worry all the time and it was always about the future. Then I decided there really isn't such a thing as the future, so why worry? All we ever have is today. Tomorrow is only an idea in your mind. Everybody reads their horoscope, goes to church, or

talks to palm readers—and nobody knows. It's a waste of time and money, and now you're doing the same thing. I'm disappointed in you Jane because I always like "Listen-In."
Jane: That's an opinion I didn't expect at the top of the show, but it is an opinion, and that's what counts. Do you ever...
Caller: I'm going to switch to another station, Jane. No offense. I love you and I like your show, but I've worried enough about the future. I'll "Listen-In" again tomorrow. What's the topic tomorrow, Jane?
Jane: Tomorrow? I'll tell you at the end of the show, OK? Thanks for your call. Goodbye. Hello, you're on "Listen-In."
Caller: Hello, I've never called you before, and I always said I wouldn't, but that man you just talked to made me mad. He said there's no future? Doesn't he read the Bible? It's *full* of the future. It says that Jesus is coming back and he will be the King in Jerusalem for a thousand years. He told us in the Bible that...
Jane: Do you know where that is in the Bible?
Caller: No, but I could find it. I've been reading this book. It's great! It makes the Bible so clear. The man who wrote it gave a talk downtown, and I bought his books after the meeting. This one is called *The Late Great Planet Earth*. It makes the future so plain that it's scary! But there are some parts everybody should read. Got a minute, Jane?
Jane: Yes, if it's not too...

Caller: I really like this part:

> For God unconditionally promised Abraham's descendants a literal world-wide kingdom over which they would rule through their Messiah....
>
> It is promised that Jerusalem will be the spiritual center of the entire world and that all people of the earth will come annually to worship Jesus who will rule there.... The Jewish believing remnant will be the spiritual leaders of the world and teach all nations the ways of the Lord.
>
> ...All men will have plenty and be secure. There will be a chicken in every pot and no one will steal it! The Great Society which human rulers throughout the centuries have promised, but never produced, will at last be realized under Christ's rule.
>
> Hal Lindsey, *The Late Great Planet Earth*, p. 165

Jane: That sounds like a combination of Franklin Roosevelt and Lyndon Johnson. I'm glad you have hope for the future, but we have other calls waiting. Thanks for letting us "Listen-In." Goodbye. Hello, you're on "Listen-In."

Caller: Hi, I'm calling about the future?

Jane: Thanks for calling. Go ahead. What about the future?

Caller: Well, I hope there is one. My girlfriend and I talk about getting married, but she doesn't want to. I tell her we have to think about the future, but she says that's why she doesn't want to get married. Do you think we should get married or just live together? What do you think, Jane?

Jane: Well, if you really love each other...

Caller: That's what I always say. Thanks, Jane, I'll tell her you said so. Goodbye.

Jane: Hello, we're "Listen-In."

Caller: Yes, hello, I want to say something about what that man said. He talked about Jesus coming back and ruling for a thousand years in Jerusalem?

Jane: Yes, do you believe that?

Caller: Yes, but he left out the really important things that are starting to happen right now. We can see the future happening already in Israel. In 1948 the Jews got control of the land. In 1967 they got control of the city of Jerusalem. Any time now we'll be hearing that they're starting to rebuild the temple and get the old worship going again. So many things have happened that we really have to watch out.

Jane: For what?

Caller: For the rapture! It can happen any minute. It may even happen in the middle of your show.

Jane: What's the rapture?

Caller: It's Christ taking all Christians who ever lived or are now living to meet him in the air. It will be the greatest trip ever taken! And it's free!

Jane: I hope you're not driving down the freeway when that happens.

Caller: Did you read the book, Jane? Rev. Lindsey has that in the book. I have that part learned almost by heart. He tells us what people will say when they are left behind and Jesus takes his believers to meet him:

"There I was, driving down the freeway and all of a sudden the place went crazy...cars going in all directions...and not one of them had a driver. I mean it was wild! I think we've got an invasion from outer space."

"It was the last quarter of the championship game and the other side was ahead. Our boys had the ball. We made a touchdown and tied it up. The crowd went crazy. Only one minute to go and they fumbled—our quarterback recovered—he was about a yard from the goal when—zap—no more quarterback—completely gone, just like that!"

Hal Lindsey, *The Late Great Planet Earth,* p. 124

Jane: That does sound spectacular, all right. Does that give you hope for the future?

Caller: Of course. Leaving the messed-up world behind is the best hope we have. I'd like to tell more about...

Jane: And we'd like to hear more, but we have to take a break. The world is messed up, but we still have to pay the light bill. We'll be back to "Listen-In" on what you say about the future after this message. We "Listen-In" when you call 633-3336, the Golden Sound of radio, WNOW.
(commercial)

We can skip the commercial and take a minute to see what's behind this talk about the future. The readings from one of Hal Lindsey's books represent a premillennial belief about the future. That view, stripped of all its sensational elements, is that Christ will return and establish his kingdom on earth *before* (pre) his thousand year (millennial) reign. He will rule the world from Jerusalem for a thousand years before the final judgment takes place. Premillennial views have been around in some form in Christian thinking since the earliest days of the church and can be traced specifically to a literal understanding of the thousand years referred to in Revelation 20.

Hal Lindsey's premillennial views, however, are part of a larger theory of the Bible and history known as dispensationalism. Dispensationalism arranges all of history into seven dispensations or periods of time. During each dispensation God tested (will test) human obedience with a different revelation of his will.

The movement began with John N. Darby (1800–82), an ex-Anglican priest who founded groups of Christians in Ireland and England. These groups became known as "Plymouth Brethren" after the group in Plymouth, England, that Darby himself led.

Darby visited Canada and the United States seven times between 1862 and 1877 to spread his teachings. Most of his followers remained in their own churches, although some of them formed Plymouth Brethren groups. Rev. James H. Brookes, Presbyterian pastor in St. Louis for thirty-three years, was influential in promoting dispensationalism. His young convert Cyrus I. Scofield (1843–1921) studied with him and eventually wrote the famous explanatory notes for the *Scofield Reference Bible* (Oxford Press, 1909). This Bible, with its extensive notes that interpret all of Scripture in the light of the seven dispensations, has popularized the theories and spread their influence through many churches.

Jane: We're back here on "Listen-In," and we have several calls waiting. In case you just tuned in, our topic today is "The Future." I expected that we would hear more about politics, but so far most of our callers have given religious thoughts about the future. A Bible college student is waiting on the line with further thoughts about the future. Go ahead, Mark.

Mark: Yes, Jane, I've been studying the future in one of my classes, and maybe I can fill you in on some of the politics of the future. Is that what you want?

Jane: Is that what you have?

Mark: Well, actually, the Bible reveals a lot of political history that hasn't happened yet. Those other callers talked about the rapture and the millennium, but it's what will happen in the seven years before the millennium that is politically explosive.

Jane: What will happen?

Mark: First there will be an alliance between Israel and the new Roman Empire. The head of the new Roman Empire will be the anti-Christ. He will declare himself God and will oppose all who believe in Christ. He will even command people to worship him in the newly rebuilt Jewish temple. When that happens, the stage is set for political upheaval.

Jane: What will happen then?

Mark: Well, the Bible says the Arab–African states will attack Israel. Then Russia will attack the Middle East from land and sea and destroy the Arab–African army. But Russia will become alarmed by reports that Red China is preparing an attack and will get set for a counterattack. Then nuclear war will break out. The Roman alliance, which probably includes the United States, will rain bombs and utterly wipe Russia out. That will set the stage for the final battle that will bring worldwide destruction. That battle between China and Rome will be centered in Israel. Just when it looks like no one will survive, Jesus will return with all the people who were caught up in the rapture and will set up his millennial

45

kingdom in Jerusalem. That will be a great day, Jane.

Jane: It almost sounds like science fiction.

Mark: But it's the gospel truth, Jane.

Jane: Is there any hope for the future?

Mark: The good news is that after the Christians are raptured to heaven and all this political and military action is getting underway, God will turn 144,000 Jews into evangelists for Jesus. I like the way Hal Lindsey says it: There are going to be 144,000 Jewish Billy Grahams turned loose on this earth—the earth will never know a period of evangelism like this period. These Jewish people are going to make up for lost time" (*The Late Great Planet Earth,* p. 99). There's a lot more, Jane, but after Christ reigns for a thousand years, the final judgment will come and Jesus will make a new heaven and a new earth. It's all in the Bible. All you have to do is put together what Zechariah, Isaiah, Ezekiel, Daniel, Paul, and Revelation say and you'll get the picture. Just read the Bible.

Jane: Can Congress do anything about it?

Mark: I don't think you understand, Jane, but I'll send you a copy of the book, OK?

Jane: Nice talking to you, Mark. Thanks for letting us "Listen-In." Goodbye. Hello, I'm Jane on WNOW and this is "Listen-In."

Caller: Yes, Jane, talking about the future, my neighbor said that they're going to open a new Sears downtown. Have you heard anything about that?

Jane: I haven't heard about it myself, but maybe we can put you in touch. . . .

While Jane tries to discover Sears' future downtown, we will attempt to trace the seven dispensations outlined in the *Scofield Reference Bible.* A dispensation, remember, is a period of time during which God tests human obedience in a specific way. Scofield discovered seven periods, each with a specific test:

1. *Innocence*
   God gave Adam commandments and prohibited the eating of one tree.
2. *Conscience*
   Sin awakened human conscience by which humankind was called to live. Disobedience brought the flood.
3. *Human Government*
   After the flood, God tested human obedience with human government. This dispensation remains in effect for the non-Jewish world until the millennium.
4. *Promise*
   This dispensation began with the call of Abraham to whom God gave great promises. It lasted until Israel reached Mt. Sinai.
5. *Law*
   The covenant made through Moses at Sinai was for Israel only and extended until the death of Christ.
6. *Grace*
   This present dispensation began after the death and resurrection of Christ and extends until the millennial kingdom. Accepting or rejecting Christ is the test of obedience.
7. *Kingdom*
   The final dispensation will be Christ's thousand-year reign in Jerusalem on the throne of David. Israel will be gathered into the kingdom, and Christ will rule over all the earth.

46

According to Scofield, we live in the dispensation of grace, between the resurrection of Christ and the millennial kingdom. According to Hal Lindsey, the way from the dispensation of grace to the dispensation of the kingdom is the bloody great tribulation.

Are these men right? If so, the events they say the Bible predicts may soon begin to take place. How much *does* the Bible tell us about the future? What's ahead?

FOR FURTHER READING

Boer, Harry R. *The Book of Revelation.* Grand Rapids, Mich.: Wm. B. Eerdmans Pub. Co., 1979.

A well-written commentary on the last book of the Bible; clearly explains the symbolism of each chapter.

Boersma, T. *Is the Bible a Jigsaw Puzzle?* St. Catharines, Ont.: Paideia Press, 1978.

A critical evaluation of Lindsey's "jigsaw puzzle" approach to the Bible with contrasting Reformed interpretation of various scriptural prophecies.

Hoekema, Anthony A. *The Bible and the Future.* Grand Rapids, Mich.: Wm. B. Eerdmans Pub. Co., 1979.

A thorough, scholarly study of eschatology (the last things) which analyzes and critiques the main current points of view on this subject.

Vanderwaal, C. *Hal Lindsey and Biblical Prophecy.* St. Catharines, Ont.: Paideia Press, 1978.

A critical study of Lindsey's use of biblical prophecy to "see inside information about the near future."

SESSION GUIDE

CHALLENGE 3   WHAT'S AHEAD?

A. Personal notes/questions on Challenge 3

B. For reading and reflection

The view of the future outlined by Lindsey relies on numerous passages from Ezekiel, Joel, Daniel, Revelation, and Matthew. Two of the most basic are Matthew 24:4–8, 29–32, 36–44 and Revelation 20. Please read these passages before doing section C below.

C. The end of the world—Reformed views versus dispensational views.

1. Using the Bible passages and Challenge 3, sequence the following events as Lindsey and others like him believe they will happen:

_____ a. The creation of a new heaven and a new earth.

_____ b. The millennium—a thousand-year reign of Christ, centered in Jerusalem and characterized by a paradiselike peace and prosperity.

_____ c. The complete restoration of the state of Israel and the rebuilding of the temple in Jerusalem.

_____ d. The tribulation—a seven-year period of worldwide war and destruction, dominated by the anti-Christ. During this time the Jews will be exalted— 144,000 of them will be converted and will work to evangelize an evil world.

_____ e. The final judgment of all unbelievers.

_____ f. The rapture—in which all believers, dead and alive, are changed and snatched from the world to meet Christ in mid-air, thus escaping the tribulation.

_____ g. The public return of Christ just at the time when it seems the world will destroy itself. Unlike the return of Christ at the rapture, this return is witnessed by all people everywhere.

_____ h. Toward the end of the millennium, Satan leads a brief insurrection which Christ crushes.

2. What questions could we raise about the way in which Lindsey has interpreted the passages from Matthew and Revelation? How do Reformed people traditionally tend to interpret these passages?

3. What events would be included in a Reformed view of the end times?

D. Evaluation

1. Accepting Lindsey's view has certain serious consequences. Think, for example, of what his view means for
   a. the way we use the Bible.
   b. why we are saved.
   c. the oneness of all people in Jesus (Gal. 3:28).
   d. the role of the church.

2. What do you think our attitude should be toward those who hold views similar to Lindsey's?

E. Faith-response

How does the knowledge of God's creation and providence help us?
We can be patient when things go against us,
   thankful when things go well,
   and for the future we can have
   good confidence in our faithful God and Father
   that nothing will separate us from his love.
All creatures are so completely in his hand
      that without his will
      they can neither move nor be moved.

Heidelberg Catechism Q & A 28

CHALLENGE 4

FOR OR AGAINST?

Belief in [Jesus Christ] and loyalty to his cause involves men in the double movement from world to God and from God to world. Even when theologies fail to do justice to this fact, Christians living with Christ in their cultures are aware of it. For they are forever being challenged to abandon all things for the sake of God; and forever being sent back into the world to teach and practice all the things that have been commanded them.

H. Richard Niebuhr, *Christ and Culture,* p. 29

Will someone kindly tell me,
  will someone let me know,
    when the FBI starts
its all-out war
  on the Ku Klux Klan?

    When we read of the Grand Wizard
seeking refuge
  in Algiers or Cuba,
    then we'll know that America
is waking up to equality.

Mary Roger Thibodeaux, S.B.S., "A Black Nun Looks at Black Power,"
Mission Trends No. 4: Liberation Theologies, p. 162

Whatever the case may be, when a revolutionary situation develops every effort must be made to achieve a nonviolent revolution. All our efforts must be directed to change without violence. But are there not extreme cases where the violence of the established order is so endemic that it necessitates a counter-violence to destroy it as soon as possible?

André Biéler, *The Politics of Hope,* p. 129

But in that obedience which we have shown to be due the authority of rulers, we are always to make this exception, indeed, to observe it as primary, that such obedience is never to lead us away from obedience to him, to whose will the desires of all kings ought to be subject, to whose decrees all their commands ought to yield, to whose majesty their scepters ought to be submitted. And how absurd would it be that in satisfying men you should incur the displeasure of him for whose sake you obey men themselves?

John Calvin, *Institutes* IV, xxii, 22

Two societies are prominent in the biblical witness. There is Babylon, and there is also Jerusalem.

Babylon is the city of death, Jerusalem is the city of salvation; Babylon, the dominion of alienation, babel, slavery, war, Jerusalem, the community of reconciliation, sanity, freedom, peace; Babylon, the harlot, Jerusalem, the bride of God; Babylon, the realm of demons and foul spirits, Jerusalem, the dwelling place in which all creatures are fulfilled; Babylon, an abomination to the Lord, Jerusalem, the holy nation; Babylon, doomed, Jerusalem, redeemed.

William Stringfellow, *An Ethic for Christians and Other Aliens in a Strange Land,* p. 34

[Stringfellow]. . .fails to note some positive tendencies in American life which, if taken into account, cast doubt on his identification of the United States with Babylon. For example, even granting the idolatrous and oppressive patterns he points to in American life, the United States has also provided in recent decades an arena for what appears to be an unprecedented and unparalleled discussion and critique of those very patterns. One wonders just who is to be identified with Babylonian America. Those members of Congress who have acted to curtail abuses of executive power, or who have exposed highly questionable "intelligence" practices? All of the black mayors of American cities? Magazines of the religious "establishment" whose pages have portrayed the hunger and suffering of the Third World?

Richard J. Mouw, *Politics and the Biblical Drama,* p. 126

As a final point, I would submit to you that the real strength of America is its religious tradition. I am concerned that too many people have lost sight of the fact that America is what it is today because God has blessed this land. Too many people today are willing to act as if God had nothing whatsoever to do with it. They don't even want to mention Him anymore. This country was built on a religious heritage, and we'd better get back to it. We had better start telling people that faith in God is the real strength of America!

Richard De Vos, *Believe!,* p. 94

One month before election day the Metropolitan Area Church Council (MACC) released the following news bulletin:

The Metropolitan Area Church Council took a stand today favoring two proposals that will be placed before the voters on Tuesday, November 5. The first—Proposal C—would establish a Metropolitan Transit Authority to purchase the ailing Stream Line Bus Company. Without public ownership the company will not be able to provide the needed services to the citizens who depend on a mass transit system. Rising costs of operating the buses have forced the company to cut back on scheduled routes that have provided primary transportation for many low-income and senior citizens. MACC spokespersons urge church members and other citizens of good will to vote YES on Proposal C.

Proposal D would increase the city income tax from 1.5 percent to 2 percent. Since city tax rules exempt $2,000 per dependent from taxation, the proposed increase will not affect those who are the least able to pay. Revenues from the increase will secure low-interest, long-term loans for homeowners who qualify for assistance under Project Renew. With the additional funds, officials estimate that 25 percent of the city's owner-occupied housing units can be restored to existing codes rather than face condemnation proceedings in the next twenty years. MACC believes that all citizens will benefit from the approval of Proposal D.

On All Saints' Day, Thursday, October 31 a public hearing will be chaired by the Rev. Caleb Schneider, pastor of the Resurrection Lutheran Church (LCA), at Our Lady of Sorrows Catholic Church on City Square. Interested citizens will hear a review of the candidates and the issues that call for decision on Tuesday, November 5. The open discussion will encourage all citizens to vote as informed, conscientious participants in the election.

All Saints' Day dawned to the ominous prediction of an unseasonal snowstorm. By midafternoon the forecast was revised and called for only two to three inches of wet snow by morning. The damage, however, was done. At the appointed hour only five citizens were scattered in the first six rows of the church basement. The number of chairs and the size of the coffee urns looked like MACC had expected about a hundred people.

Rev. Schneider suggested that the agenda be set aside in favor of an informal discussion over coffee. The plan for the evening had anticipated breaking up into small groups anyway. The introductions revealed that all five persons in attendance were active members of different churches. Rev. Schneider, who preferred to be called by his first name, Caleb, invited an open discussion to answer the question, "How should Christians vote next Tuesday?" The discussion was lively.

Agnes McNary: Before we talk about how Christians should vote, I think we should talk about the most important factor in any election in this great city.

Caleb: What is the most important factor?

Agnes: Getting every registered voter to the polls! It's too late now to work on getting people registered. That's really the first thing. Now we have to work at getting all the registered voters to the polls. It's a shame that in most elections we get only 25 to 40 percent of the voters to the polls. If we hit 60 percent it's almost a record. How can we get God's will done if all the voters don't vote? We can discuss what God wants for our city all we please, but if people don't vote, we'll never know. God has put a little of his Spirit in everyone; the trouble is that people don't vote. If everyone went to the polls, we'd see a new society. We'd see Jesus working in our city. If anyone was for democracy, Jesus was. We shouldn't spend time discussing the issues if we're not going to help get the voters to the polls.

Jason Johnson: I can't believe what I'm hearing. I didn't come here to say any-

thing, but under the circumstances I can't keep quiet. I came here to do a report for our *Fellowship News* and to see if our city is really in as great a mess as I think it is. I believe Christians shouldn't vote at all. I think we should quietly boycott the election. The most important "election" in history, the vote between Jesus and Barabbas, went against Jesus. It's no different now. Government is always self-serving, no matter how big the smile it wears. I believe Christians should just ignore the election and go about what matters: praying, witnessing, and building Christian communities in this wasteland. Let the politicians play their games. If we do anything for government, it should be to expose their real interests through nonviolent protests. Election day just misleads people into thinking it's *their* government. If you take a pile of garbage and rearrange it, put it in a different package, and tie it with a different ribbon, it's still garbage. Government is corrupt, and election day is just a nice way of packaging it. I think that if we want to follow Christ, we should walk *away* from the polls.

Caleb: I'm sorry about the snowstorm, but it surely isn't cold in here. If I hear you right, we have a difference of opinion. It's good that we can be so open and honest about our feelings and still respect each other.

David Carpenter: That all sounds rather extreme. I think Christians should vote like any citizen should vote: we should think the issues through, listen to the candidates, and use our common sense. Christians don't have more insight than anyone else when it comes to voting. At least, I certainly haven't noticed that being a Christian makes anyone a more expert citizen or voter than anyone else. In fact, I think some atheists are more intelligent voters than some Christians.

Caleb: Do you think Christians have more faith, hope, and love than people who don't live by the teachings of the Bible?

David: Yes, but that's quite personal and it doesn't automatically make us better voters. I'm a

member of Our Lady of Sorrows here, and I attend mass regularly. Before I became a Christian, I lived the best life I could. I probably knew more about politics then than I do now. I was a devoted citizen, but something was missing from my life. What I receive now in the holy eucharist, the world could not give and cannot take away. But I don't vote much differently now than I did before I became a Catholic. In fact, I think it's dangerous to our spiritual life to mix the meaning of the mass with voting. It takes faith to attend mass; it takes common sense to go to the polls.

Caleb: David, do you mind saying how you are going to vote on C and D?

David: I think I'll vote yes on the transit Proposal C and no on the tax increase, Proposal D. Public support for mass transit is very important, but our housing problems won't be solved by taxation. The tax and Project Renew will just obscure the real housing problems.

Susan Van Dyk: I'm planning to vote just the opposite, David. I'm against city ownership of the bus lines and I'm for the income tax increase. The tax increase won't hurt the poor and it *will* help the city maintain our housing stock. The biggest problem in this city in the next years will be housing. It's also the biggest expense that anyone faces. And when housing deteriorates, it hurts the most helpless. Transportation is important, but city ownership of the bus lines will still price bus rides out of reach of the poor. I would rather see us regulate the bus lines and subsidize the poor who need transportation. Housing is more important than transportation right now, and I think we should keep first things first.

Caleb: Do you take that position because of your common sense, as David talked about it, or because of your faith?

Susan: Well, I believe that Christians sort of live in two worlds. We studied that in church. It's like Christ's kingdom and our government are both there, but they're not the same. The church and city hall are always separate and they live by different rules. We have to make choices in both of them. All I can really say is that we have to do the best we can. Christ is king of the church, but if you've read the papers lately, you know he isn't running city hall!

Caleb: We haven't heard from you, James. How are you going to vote as a Christian?

James Grant: What can I say? As a Presbyterian I'm like a sheep among wolves.

Caleb: It's All Saints' Day, James, and I think even Presbyterians have had a saint or two. How will you vote on C and D?

James: Well, I'm voting for both of them because I believe those are the best choices among the options before us. I also believe Jesus is Lord without the limitations Susan sees. His will should be done by city hall as well as by the church council. The only other kingdom we have to reckon with besides the kingdom of Christ is the kingdom of evil, and that kingdom attacks the church as frequently as it attacks city hall. Voting in an annual church meeting is no different than voting in a city election. Voting, like everything else we do, must serve Christ as Lord.

Caleb: That doesn't say why you're voting for C and D.

James: Just look at the alternatives. You can say yes or no to C and D. Right? Those are the choices. I wish we had a few other options, but we don't. I believe that saying yes to both proposals will make government more faithful to Christ's will than saying no. When those are your choices, that's the way to choose. We never have ideal

choices but, like I said, voting in the city isn't that different from voting in the church. Jesus is Lord, and government must be made to serve him just as the church does.

Agnes: See what I mean? David is voting yes on C and no on D. Susan is voting no on C and yes on D. James is voting yes on both. Isn't that beautiful? All those very good and thoughtful choices go into the voting machines. What's important, as I said before, is that everyone votes. Jesus' Spirit can't win anything in the city if people don't vote. It isn't *how* you vote that matters; it's *that* you vote.

Jason: And I think that's the greatest absurdity of all. Voting doesn't matter. Government is government no matter who wins or loses. It's all much ado about nothing. What *is* important is that we live in Christian fellowship and prayer and follow Christ as our example. Who wins an election is no more important than who wins the world series.

David: I think we should use our common sense in voting and not get politics confused with the liturgy and sacraments of the church. At the polls we're just citizens. At mass we're children of God.

Susan: Let God be God and let Caesar be Caesar. That's the effect of what Jesus said. It gets tricky sometimes, but living with one foot in Christ's kingdom and the other foot in this city is not simple. It never was. You just have to do the best you can to find your way in both kingdoms.

James: I feel uncertain sometimes about what's the best or the right thing to do, but I'm sure Jesus is as much the Lord of the city as he is of the church. I had to be converted to his service. So does business, labor, government, and education. When election day comes, you just have to say yes or no in the light of what serves him best. Until we get a different way of doing it, that's the way to vote. And incidentally, I think Christians should keep working at reforming the systems so that they will be better instruments of Christ's justice, peace, and order.

Caleb: It's snowing again. The buses stopped running about an hour ago. Does anyone need a ride home? Or, if you want to stay, we still have four gallons of coffee.

FOR FURTHER READING

Kuyper, Abraham. *Lectures on Calvinism.* Grand Rapids, Mich.: Associated Publishers and Authors, Inc., 1932.

These so-called Stone Lectures given at Princeton in 1898 remain one of the best, brief assertions of Christ's claims over every sphere of life.

Leith, John H. *Introduction to the Reformed Tradition.* Atlanta: John Knox Press, 1977.

Chapter 7, "Culture and the Reformed Tradition," gives a clear exposition of the Reformed and Presbyterian position on Christianity and Culture.

Mouw, Richard J. *Politics and the Biblical Drama.* Grand Rapids, Mich.: Wm. B. Eerdmans Pub. Co., 1976.

Concentrating more particularly on the area of politics, this book delineates the "kingly" task of the Christian community.

Niebuhr, Richard H. *Christ and Culture.* New York: Harper & Row, 1951.

This book remains the most comprehensive and basic exposition of the five alternate views of Christ and culture.

weak
- traditional
- (old-fashioned)
- evangalising
- new people
- positive outlooks

formality

SESSION GUIDE

CHALLENGE 4   FOR OR AGAINST?

A. Personal notes/questions on Challenge 4

Assignment :

Where, when, how why

Write what I think C.C.R. churches strength
are, what are its weaknesses ! !
     2 pages : GRRRRRRR !!
             yucky!

B. Five votes, five points of view

1. If you had to vote on Proposals C and D, which position would you take—that of Agnes, Jason, David, Susan, or James? Why?

I am not of age to vote.

2. How do the five people listed above see the relationship between the church and city hall, or between Christ and culture?

Agnes—

Jason— *not at all*

David— *yes on C   NO on D*

Susan— *NO on C   yes on D*

James— *yes on C   yes on D*

3. Match each of the five people to one of the following views of Christ and culture, as given by H. Richard Niebuhr in *Christ and Culture.*

Christ of culture

Christ above culture

Christ the transformer of culture

Christ and culture in paradox

Christ against culture

4. Although all five of the Christ and culture views can be valid under certain circumstances, many Christians tend to identify with just one of the five views. For example, which do you think is the modern liberal view? Which the view of such Anabaptist groups as the Hutterites? Which the Reformed/Presbyterian view? Which the Catholic view? The Lutheran view?

5. If you were asked to defend the Reformed/Presbyterian view of Christ as transformer of culture, what would you say? In other words, why do we support *this* view?

(probably wouldn't say anything. I'd just follow whats supposed to be right. and do what I'm supposed to.)

C. Application

Proposals C and D were lifelike but fictional issues. Substitute a real local or national issue and show how a Reformed view of Christ as transformer of culture could affect your involvement and your position.

D. Confessional/biblical resources

The members of the church are emissaries of peace and seek the good of man in cooperation with the powers and authorities in politics, culture, and economics. But they have to fight against pretensions and injustices when these same powers endanger human welfare.

Confession of 1967, I, C, 1 (Presbyterian)

"All authority in heaven and on earth has been given to me. Go therefore and make disciples of all nations...teaching them to observe all that I have commanded you."

Matthew 28:18–20

Do not be conformed to this world but be transformed by the renewal of your mind, that you may prove what is the will of God, what is good and acceptable and perfect.

Romans 12:2

AM I SAVED?

It must be admitted that people who have had sudden conversions sometimes exaggerate their sharpness. . . . Before they were converted they never had a pure thought, hated God, and planned on poisoning all their sisters. But since 9:47 on Tuesday the 24th, they have been singing all day long and have opened three Christian bookstores.

Cornelius Plantinga Jr., *Beyond Doubt,* leader's guide, p. 54

The Christian doctrine of salvation is the focus of intense debate in the Church today. Contributing to the confusion is unclarity about the word "save." It is taken from a common usage that often means the accumulation or preservation of things, from money in the bank to time on a clock. The meaning of the term in the Scriptures and tradition of the Church is otherwise. In these contexts it is used in two other ways. On the one hand, to be saved means to be rescued or delivered from a foe. On the other hand, it signifies healing or making whole. Thus we are saved *from* something and saved *for* something.

Gabriel Fackre, *The Christian Story,* p. 182

When the Son of God came to us clothed in flesh, he received from the Father a name which plainly told for what purpose he came, what was his power, and what we had a right to expect from him.

John Calvin, *Commentary* on Matthew 1:21

There are times for most believers when all the zest has gone out of the Christian faith. It does not mean much to us at the moment, and we know it. Prayer is a bore. We are weary in well-doing. Preaching is powerless to move us. We wonder if the whole Christian enterprise has not been a sadly human mistake.

Cornelius Plantinga Jr., *A Place to Stand,* p. 158

"And there is salvation in no one else, for there is no other name under heaven given among men by which we must be saved."

Acts 4:12

Question Mark

The Reverend Mark Mc Callum D.D.

Last month the following letter was received from "Troubled in Providence." Along with my advice I invited readers to respond to his question and to offer counsel. Question Mark has never before received such a volume of response. The last count showed 263 letters had arrived in 27 days—approximately ten per day. Because the question tapped a deep well of concern in the evangelical Christian community, the letter is republished here with four representative responses. No further letters of reply will be published, but all letters addressed to Troubled, c/o Question Mark, have been and will be forwarded.

M.M.

Dear Mark:

Three months ago I would have bet my life that I would never write you. But that was before I bet my life on the deal that couldn't lose. That makes me a two-time loser. The narcs won then and you win now.

Am I saved? That's as plain as I can say it. It isn't just because I'm in County Jail and probably face some hard time; I ask because I thought I was saved three times before, and now it may be happening again. But before I go any farther, I need to know if I *can* be saved and how I can *know* if I am.

The first time I was only eight. I heard the story of Zacchaeus in an afterschool Bible class and immediately identified with him: I was small too. So when the teacher (who looked like an angel) asked if we wanted to accept Jesus into our house and heart, I said I did. For a few months after that I was a changed person. I helped with the dishes without being asked and even let my little brother Joey beat me in a game of ping-pong. I thought that would win God's favor forever.

I got over that "conversion" after summer vacation. But I still think I was very sincere at the time.

When I was fifteen, I was "saved" for the second time. Several churches had a retreat at a church youth camp. My purpose in attending had nothing to do with the purpose of the retreat. I could have cared less about religion then. But after I had challenged the Bible leader that night without mercy, I was changed.

One of the group climbed the big stone fireplace in the lodge and put my wallet fourteen feet from the floor on a ledge. They dared me to get it. I tried. I couldn't. They laughed. The leader watched. When he saw I was about to break under rage and frustration, he scaled the fireplace like a veteran climber while everyone watched in stunned silence. It was dramatic. With his arms spread against the stone, it looked like he could have been on a cross. He dropped my wallet to me, climbed down, grinned, and walked away.

I followed him. That night we talked in his room. I accepted Christ again, and he prayed as though he had expected it. I will never forget that evening.

That was '68. In the months that followed came the riots, the worst of Vietnam, and Watergate. My salvation wore off. The deaths at Kent State happened the month I graduated from high school. I saw no hope, and stopped looking.

The third time I "found Jesus" was after I met Linda. She attended the Academy for Christian Studies led by campus ministers at the university. One evening after a C. S. Lewis study seminar we attended together, I made a quiet but clear commitment. This time I was sure I gave my life to God, and the gospel made sense to me in a way it hadn't before.

But after breaking up with Linda and graduating from the university, I couldn't find a job. I read a lot and started driving a cab. God didn't seem very real anymore. In a weak moment I agreed to make the drop at a downtown motel for some friends. It was only a small package, but it contained a sizable quantity of hash and cocaine. It would have "earned" me enough to pay my rent for six months. Of course, I don't *have* to pay the rent now. The narcs were waiting. I've waived the preliminary exam and

will stand trial soon.

The chaplain here visited last night. He doesn't feel sorry for me at all, but he cares. He listened and talked about a new beginning. I've had new beginnings before, and look where I am now.

Like the other times, I really want to be saved. Can I? How can I be sure?

Troubled in Providence

Reply 1

Dear Troubled:

Your story is like mine in a hundred ways! After I had accepted Christ for the twelfth time, I would lie awake at night thinking about my sincerity. But since I could never be sure about my sincerity, I gave it up.

My problem was that I tried to find the assurance of salvation in myself, and it was never there. What changed that for me was the power of holy baptism and holy communion. Sure, I still believe that the Word of God is enough to bring us salvation, but God

knows most of us can't have assurance without the sacraments! Isn't that what baptism and communion are for?

Were you baptized? If not, I recommend it and Christ expects it. Get baptized and then attend every baptism you can. I was baptized when I was only three weeks old and don't remember a thing about it, but I have heard the story of my birth and baptism many times. Now every time I see a baptism, it's as though I'm in it. It's like a new beginning for me each time. Baptism has given me confidence in Christ.

And holy communion has been an unending source of certainty. The words are like arrows of grace that stab my uncertainty: "My body for you," "My blood for you." They make Christ real now. The words, the action, the taste, the smell, the people—and the Spirit who brings it all together into an experience of assurance.

I plead with you to stop looking inside yourself to find assurance that you can be saved. You won't find it there. Don't miss the joy and reality of baptism and communion. They make salvation real in ways nothing else can. When baptism and communion happen, you will *know* Christ is there.

It sounds like you'll be in jail for a while. That could be hard, but it's not necessarily bad. Jail may be the smallest part of your problem. Some great New Testament saints did time, although for different reasons. I'm praying that you will find assurance.
W. B. in Centerburg

Reply 2
Dear Troubled:
When I read your letter, my whole life passed before me. My whole life, that is, until May 16 of last year. That day I experienced salvation in a way I never did before, and so can you.

It was Friday evening and some friends invited me to a meeting. I hadn't been to a church for a while because I couldn't relate to the churches I knew. So they asked me to come to their Pulse

night, but since then I've never doubted it. I *know* I'm saved. I have assurance for the first time in memory.

If I was out of bondage before that day, I surely wasn't in the Promised Land. I was wandering in the wilderness of doubt and uncertainty.

The Spirit of Christ is now the center of my faith and the Pulse group is the center of my life. I never lack the assurance of salvation. Week after week I am growing in faith and in experience with the Lord. Our Pulse group prayed for you last time, and the Lord showed us that one of us should visit you. You can expect one of us to come soon. Once you experience the heartbeat of the body of Christ and hear the voice of the Spirit, you will never have to be saved again. You will *know*.

In the Spirit,
E. D. in Albany

Reply 3

Dear Troubled:

Yes, you can be saved. Anyone can. That's the good news. Why? Because about two thousand years ago Jesus Christ sacrificed himself on the cross for the sins of the world. That includes you. The third day he arose victoriously from the dead and is now ascended at the right hand of the Father.

It sounds like your trust in him is sincere, but you are looking in your own heart and life for the assurance of salvation rather than looking to him.

I'm going to be perfectly frank: your story is monotonous. I've heard it and even told it a thousand times. You can change this detail, or that, but it's the same monotonous,

group. I asked what that meant. And they explained that the church was supposed to be the body of Christ, right? Right! I had learned that in Catechism. Well, they call their group Pulse because when they gather they feel the heartbeat of the body of Christ. They told me churches are like dead skeletons; they formed Pulse so they could feel the life of Christ.

And wow! I could feel that life right away. The leader opened the Bible to help us get into the Word. Everyone shared what the Lord had done for them and was doing for them. Toward the end of the evening they asked me what the Lord had done for me. All I could think to say was, "He brought me here tonight."

That started it. They praised the Lord right there—for me! They prayed with their hands on me. One person started speaking in a language he didn't know and I didn't understand. I can't say I was saved that human story. The only story that's unique, always new, and always good is the story of Jesus. Get your story out of the way of *his* story and you will find assurance in him.

Say the Apostle's Creed daily. Listen for the story in it—God's grand story that is still going on. Put yourself into that creed and hold on to all the promises that are there. All other assurances crumble.

Christ's story matters, not yours. Stories about the experience of other Christians can hurt as well as help. Salvation comes from his death and resurrection, or it doesn't come at all.

We have his word for that. All other ground is sinking sand.

Confidently,
J. S. in Des Moines

Reply 4

Dear Troubled:

I have one simple bit of advice for you: if you want to be saved, start serving Christ right where you are. It doesn't matter how many good or evil works you've done in the past. It doesn't matter how much you know, how much you've experienced, or how many decisions you've made for Christ. What matters is whether you love and serve Christ today.

People get mixed up about that. If everyone waited until they had full assurance of salvation to get with doing the will of Christ in the world (even in jail), we would all wait forever. It's in serving Christ and our neighbor that assurance comes. It's by losing yourself in love for others that Christ gives confidence.

Is there a letter you should have written before? Is there someone in jail who needs a friend, some encouragement, or a word of witness? Is there someone (maybe even a guard!) whose feet need washing (John 13)? Do it. Assurance comes as a quiet gift.

If you don't serve, you won't grow in faith or assurance. That's what salvation is all about. And remember: "He who loves is born of God and knows God" (1 John 4:7). Isn't that a grand assurance?

In Christ,
M. D. in Pensacola

FOR FURTHER READING

Bavinck, Herman. *The Certainty of Faith.* St. Catharines, Ont.: Paideia Press, 1980.

> Beginning with a contrast between the certainty of science and the certainty of religion, this book reviews historically the ways to certainty and concludes by asserting the indispensable role of certainty in the Christian faith.

Berkouwer, G. C. *Faith and Perseverance.* Grand Rapids, Mich.: Wm. B. Eerdmans Pub. Co., 1958.

> In this thorough theological study of the doctrine of the perseverance of the saints, the last chapter ("The Reality of Perseverance") gives some valuable pastoral advice.

Plantinga, Cornelius, Jr. *A Place to Stand.* Grand Rapids, Mich.: Board of Publications of the Christian Reformed Church, 1979.

> Chapter 31, entitled "The Perseverance of the Saints," explains clearly the Canons of Dort teachings (Fifth Head of Doctrine) about the assurance of salvation.

SESSION GUIDE

CHALLENGE 5   AM I SAVED?

A. Personal notes/questions on Challenge 5

B. Replies to Troubled in Providence

Working with others in your group, decide which one of the four replies in Challenge 5 offers the best advice to Troubled in Providence. Should you find that none of the replies are very helpful, briefly outline what you think a good Reformed reply would say.

Please read session guide section *D* before your group discussion. During your discussion, keep this question in mind: what is, finally, our only hope and assurance of salvation?

C. Questions for additional discussion

1. Must we have a conversion experience in order to be saved? Explain.

2. What is meant by the perseverance of the saints? (See excerpts from Canons of Dort in section *D*.) How does this thoroughly Reformed teaching assure us of our salvation?

3. If our salvation is so firmly in the hands of almighty God and rests on his faithfulness, why are Christians sometimes uncertain about their salvation? What can be done about this uncertainty if we are caught in it?

4. What Scripture passages come to mind as reassurances that we do belong to Christ and are saved?

D. Confessional resources

Excerpt from Canons of Dort, Fifth Head of Doctrine, Articles 3, 8, 9, and 10:

By reason of these remains of indwelling sin, and also because of the temptations of the world and of Satan, those who are converted could not persevere in that grace if left to their own strength. But God is faithful, who, having conferred grace, mercifully confirms and powerfully preserves them therein, even to the end....

Thus it is not in consequence of their own merits or strengths, but of God's free mercy, that they neither totally fall from faith and grace nor...perish....God's council cannot be changed nor His promise fail....

True believers themselves may and do obtain assurance according to the measure of their faith....

This assurance, however, is not produced by any peculiar revelation contrary to or independent of the Word of God, but springs from faith in God's promises...from the testimony of the Holy Spirit...and...from a serious and holy desire to preserve a good conscience and to perform good works.

Westminster Confession of Faith, Chapter XIV, Article 3:

This faith is different in degrees, weak or strong; may be often and many ways assailed, but gets the victory; growing up in many to the attainment of a full assurance, through Christ, who is both the author and finisher of our faith.

Q & A 1 of the Heidelberg Catechism:

*What is your only comfort
in life and in death?*

That I am not my own,
but belong—
  body and soul,
  in life and in death—
to my faithful Savior Jesus Christ....

Because I belong to him,
Christ, by his Holy Spirit,
assures me of eternal life
and makes me whole-heartedly willing and ready
from now on to live for him.

WHO SHOULD BE BAPTIZED?

And first baptize the little ones; and if they can speak for themselves, they shall do so; if not, their parents or other relatives shall speak for them. Then baptize the men, and last of all the women; they must first loosen their hair and put aside any gold or silver ornaments that they are wearing: let no one take any alien thing down to the water with them.

Hippolytus, *The Apostolic Tradition*, A.D. 215–17

If it is reasonable for children to be brought to Christ, why is it not allowable to admit them to baptism, the symbol of our communion and fellowship with Christ? ...How unjust shall we be if we drive away from Christ those whom he invites to him; if we deprive them of the gifts with which he adorns them; if we exclude those whom he freely admits!

John Calvin, *Institutes* IV, xvi, 7

If we would not maliciously obscure the kindness of God, let us present to him our infants, to whom he has assigned a place among his friends and family, that is, the members of the Church.

John Calvin, *Institutes* IV, xviii, 32

God's reconciling and regenerating work constitutes the fulfillment of the promise which lies at the heart of the covenant and of all God's dealings with his covenant people. From the very beginning the covenant carried with it the creation of a redeemed and renewed people, at first restricted in the main to a single nation but then broadened to embrace all nations. The fulfillment of the covenant in and with the death and resurrection of Jesus Christ means that the word of promise has been succeeded by the word of accomplishment, and the Old Testament signs of anticipation have been succeeded by the New Testament signs of recollection.

Geoffrey W. Bromiley, *Children of Promise,* p. 36

How was one baptized in the New Testament period? We don't really know. The rite consisted of at least two essentials: the divine name and the use of water.

Eugene L. Brand, *Baptism: A Pastoral Perspective,* p. 23

The Christian says: Baptism is my departure out of chaos into the order of the forgiven life. It is my visitation by the Spirit which broods over this water of life. It is my deliverance from the destroying floods, my passage through the Red Seas of sin and enmity. I am humbled by it as was Job, inspired by it as was the Psalmist. Baptism is my trip to the Jordan. In this water I am crucified with Christ; nevertheless I live, sharing his living water. None of these events, activities, pictures, signs, symbols, pre- or post-figurations detract from the one meaning, that here I seek and find the joy of forgiveness. Rather they are the countless colors that add riches to the full portrait. They are the grace notes that parallel God's melodic line. They are the story of my life, a life which is born in baptism. They all deal with water and with the Word of the One who restores me to life. They are my waters of Siloam and my pool of Bethesda, my entrance to the new life of the kingdom: thoughts such as these could well occupy any Christian who observes someone else's baptism.

Martin E. Marty, *Baptism,* p. 17

When Alan and Sonia Bell asked the local Anglican vicar in Nunneaton, England, to baptize their infant son, Steven, the answer they got was, "Do it yourself." Father Richard Higginbottom of Holy Trinity Church said that he refused to perform the service because the Bells were not churchgoers. He added that he had advised other couples to baptize their own children in a local stream. "The Church of England does not have a monopoly on baptisms," he commented. "Anyone can baptize anyone as long as they use the correct words and some water. If people want their children baptized by the Church of England, they must abide by the rules." The Bells had their baby baptized in a Congregational church.

The Christian Century, June 3–10, 1981, p. 633

The rippling waterway reflected the Florida sun. The large mirrored windows that flanked the entrance to New Hope Church caught the rays and created a curtain of dancing waves. Facing east and overlooking the cove, the church was known for its facade of "living water." The faithful and the tourists who entered at 10 A.M. on Sunday mornings lingered to enjoy the view and the mural painted by the sun and water. The effect was spoiled only when it rained.

Inside there was different water. The service of holy baptism was in progress.

"Donald and Amy Kendall, will you come forward and present Jill Alice for holy baptism?"

The pastor left the pulpit and stepped down to the baptismal font. An elder arose and stood beside him. Donald carried Jill as they gathered around the graceful walnut stand in full view of the whole church. Reverend Harris faced the young couple and continued to speak—this time not to God or to the congregation, but directly to the parents. Donald and Amy had witnessed many baptisms, but never at such close range. Their attention was torn between the awesome mystery of the moment and Jill's slightest twitch.

"Donald and Amy, since you have presented Jill for holy baptism, you are asked to answer the following questions before God and his people:

"First, do you confess Jesus Christ as your Lord and Savior, accept the promises of God, and affirm the truth of the Christian faith which is proclaimed in the Bible and confessed in this church of Christ?

"Second, do you believe that Jill, though sinful by nature, is received by God in Christ as a member of his covenant, and therefore ought to be baptized?

"Third, do you promise, in reliance on the Holy Spirit and with the help of the Christian community, to do all in your power to instruct her in the Christian faith and to lead her by your example into the life of Christian discipleship?"

Reverend Harris looked at Donald and Amy expectantly.

"We do, God helping us," they answered. Even with all the practice, their halting voices were not quite together. But everyone understood.

Turning to the congregation, the pastor had another question: "Do you, the people of the Lord, promise to receive Jill Alice in love, pray for her, help care for her instruction in the faith, and encourage and sustain her in the fellowship of believers?"

"We do, God helping us."

Without hesitation the elder lifted the cover, exposing the silver basin half filled with lukewarm tap water. Donald and Amy would talk often about the flood of memories the sight of the water stirred within them and the sense of wonder that came over them. The pastor dipped his hand into the basin and lifted a palmful of water for all the people to see and hear as it cascaded back into the bowl. His words reached the balcony without the help of an amplifier as he sprinkled water to the cadence of the liturgy: "Jill Alice Kendall, I baptize you in the name of the Father, of the Son, and of the Holy Spirit, Amen."

There was more. The sermon was from the story of the conversion of the jail warden in Philippi and the baptism of his household (Acts 16:25–34). The story was familiar, but Donald and Amy heard it as though it were new. They could identify with the jailer's question, drawn out of him by the faithful witness of Paul and Silas and driven out of him by fear for his life: What must I do to be saved? They rejoiced with the whole church when he cast his life on the mercy of Paul and Silas and then on the Lord Jesus Christ. They felt hope as they saw the power of the gospel and the sign of baptism bring salvation to that family. They caught the humor of a Roman warden feeding and sheltering prisoners in his own house.

Donald and Amy knew that they, like Jill, were children of God and servants of the Lord Jesus Christ.

On Tuesday morning of that same week, Reverend Harris answered the telephone in his study. "New Hope Church. May I help you?"

"Hello, Reverend Harris?"

"Yes."

"This is Claudia Williams. I don't know if you remember me, but I was in your church again last Sunday with my husband, Bradley. We're the ones with the three children and the baby, remember?"

"Yes, I remember. You've worshiped with us three times in the last month."

"Well, Sunday was just beautiful. All of us loved what happened and what you said. It was like God was speaking right to us. I'm calling to see if you can do all of us. Can we be done all at the same time?"

"Done? You mean you want to be baptized?"

"Yes, just like you said it was done to the whole family in the Bible story. That was such a good sermon. It made something clear to me for the first time. We would like it done just like you said. Do you baptize in homes?"

"Our baptisms all happen in Sunday worship at the church."

"Well, we don't know many people there

yet, but we love your church and we want to get a new start. God knows how much we need it. We've only lived here four months."

"And you have four chldren?"

"Well, sort of. Actually, Bradley and I have three children. Samuel is our adopted Korean child. He's eleven. Kevin is fifteen and Teresa is seventeen. Monica is Teresa's child and she's eighteen months. I'd rather explain later. We're quite a new family."

"It's good to hear that you love our church and want to be baptized. I think we should talk it over. Can we do that on Thursday evening at 8:30? I'll be glad to come to your home if that's convenient."

It was.

Claudia Williams had lived all of her forty-six years in western Pennsylvania. The recent move to Florida was a symbol of her search for a new future. She hoped that the many miles between her past and future would help heal the hurts and recover the dreams. The new surroundings meant new opportunity.

Although she had fought hard to save the marriage, she had been divorced for eleven years. The small town where she had grown up had done much for her during those difficult days, but even some of her close friends were divided over the custody suit. The court had awarded their nine-year-old son Alan to her ex-husband and their six-year-old daughter Teresa to her. The scandal and pain weakened her faithfulness to St. Mark's Church where she and Teresa had been baptized. The priests had encouraged and helped her but it was still hard to face the people on Sunday.

Nine years later life finally seemed to be getting better. At least until fifteen-year-old Teresa became pregnant. It was too much.

Even friends from church urged her to have an abortion, and everyone wanted the child placed for adoption. Claudia and Teresa decided they would keep the baby. Monica was theirs, and she would remain in the family.

Claudia had known Bradley Williams since high school, but they hadn't been friends since he had gone away to college. He and his first wife had two children, Kevin, now fifteen, and Samuel, age eleven. Samuel was a Korean child whom they had adopted through their church. After twenty years of marriage, Bradley was widowed. For four years he had devoted his life to raising his sons. He and Claudia met again during Teresa's pregnancy, and their friendship flourished. Their marriage was now less than two years old, but they believed deeply that God had brought them together.

The whole family was still adjusting to the new surroundings. The new home, neighborhood, and job were only a small part of their many challenges. They were still adjusting to each other and striving to overcome the pain and tragedy of the past.

They were not familiar with New Hope Church, but they recognized that their faith in Jesus Christ was proclaimed and celebrated there. They had many questions that couldn't be answered in a single visit, but they knew that God had spoken to them in the sermon of last Sunday and in the baptism of Jill Alice Kendall. Brad and Claudia agreed: they wanted to be baptized with their three children and Monica. It was part of their hope for a new beginning.

Reverend Harris spent several hours with them that evening. He wrote down the family record:

Bradley Williams, age forty-five. Baptized at age eleven at Calvary Baptist Church,

Norman, Pennsylvania. Communicant member.

Claudia Williams, age forty-six. Baptized at St. Mark's Church, Silverton, Pennsylvania. Confirmed at age twelve. Communicant member.

Teresa Watson, age seventeen. Baptized and confirmed at St. Mark's.

Monica Watson, age eighteen months. Not baptized.

Kevin Williams, age fifteen. Not baptized, but a faithful member at Calvary Baptist Sunday school. Scout Troop patrol leader.

Samuel Williams, age eleven. Not baptized, but a faithful member at Calvary Baptist Sunday school and youth choir.

Telling their stories brought some tears and some laughter. Their hope for a new future was fragile, but real. The newness all around them gave them hope tinged with fear.

Would he baptize them like Paul baptized the jailer's household?

Reverend Harris promised that he would present their request to the elders of the church, explaining that they were responsible for receiving and supervising church members. He would return to visit with an elder next week.

They sat in a circle as Reverend Harris read Ephesians 3:14–21 and prayed.

Everyone said "Amen."

FOR FURTHER READING

Berkouwer, G. C. *The Sacraments.* Grand Rapids, Mich.: Wm. B. Eerdmans Pub. Co., 1969.

> A thorough theological study of the sacraments that argues for a Reformed view of baptism against both Catholic theologians and against Karl Barth.

Bridges, Donald and Phypers, David. *The Water that Divides.* Downers Grove, Ill.: Inter-Varsity Press, 1977.

> A very readable debate over baptism written by a Baptist and an Anglican. Presents scriptural, historical, and practical arguments on both sides.

Bromiley, Geoffrey W. *Children of Promise.* Grand Rapids, Mich.: Wm. B. Eerdmans Pub. Co., 1979.

> A brief but thorough argument for infant baptism which presents both biblical and doctrinal grounds. Also includes a practical guide for churches.

Piet, John H. *The Road Ahead.* Grand Rapids, Mich.: Wm. B. Eerdmans Pub. Co., 1970.

> Chapter 7 discusses baptism as related to circumcision and as part of the church's mission.

SESSION GUIDE

CHALLENGE 6   WHO SHOULD BE BAPTIZED?

A. Personal notes/questions on Challenge 6

B. Background for the case study in Challenge 6

    1. How is baptism performed in your church (sprinkling or immersion)? Why? See Heidelberg Catechism Q & A 69 and Westminster Larger Catechism Q & A 165 (section *D*).

sprinkling

    2. Have you ever witnessed an adult baptism? If so,
        —was the adult being baptized for the first time?
        —had the adult been baptized before in another denomination?
    Is it necessary to be rebaptized when you join a new denomination? Why or why not?

yep
I don't know
I don't know

    3. Why are infants baptized in your church? (See Heidelberg Catechism Q & A 74 and/or your baptismal forms.)

So that were in Gods covenant

    4. From a Reformed perspective, which of the following makes baptism effective?
        —the place where it's done (an orthodox church)
        —the way it's done (by immersion or sprinkling)
        —the person doing it (an orthodox minister)
        —the faith of those answering the questions
        —the proper formula (in the name of Father, Son, and Holy Spirit)
        —all of the above
        —none of the above

C. Case study from Challenge 6

You and the others in your group are now serving as officers of your church. The pastor has asked you to decide whether or not the entire Williams family should be baptized as they've requested. If you decide they should, what reasons can you give the congregation for your decision? If you decide they should not, what exactly do you suggest? For example, should *some* of the family be baptized? Which ones? Should some be given a choice?

Please base your response on the facts presented in Challenge 6 and on the preliminary thinking you've done in section *B.* Refer to the creeds and forms of your church as necessary.

D. Resources

Q & A 66 of Heidelberg Catechism:

What are sacraments?

Sacraments are holy signs and seals for us to see.
They were instituted by God so that
  by our use of them
he might make us understand
  the promise of the gospel,
and might put his seal on that promise.

And this is God's gospel promise:
  to forgive our sins and give us eternal life
    by grace alone
    because of Christ's one sacrifice
    finished on the cross.

Q & A 69 of the Heidelberg Catechism:

How does baptism remind you and assure you
that Christ's one sacrifice on the cross is for you personally?

In this way:
Christ instituted the outward washing
and with it gave the promise that,
   as surely as water washes away the dirt from the body,
   so certainly his blood and his Spirit
   wash away my soul's impurity,
     in other words, all my sins.

Q & A 165 of the Westminster Larger Catechism:

What is Baptism?

Baptism is a sacrament of the New Testament, wherein Christ hath ordained the washing with water . . . to be a sign and a seal of ingrafting into himself, of remission of sins by his blood, and regeneration by his Spirit; of adoption, and resurrection unto everlasting life. . . .

Q & A 74 of the Heidelberg Catechism:

Should infants, too, be baptized?

Yes.
Infants as well as adults
   are in God's covenant and are his people.
They, no less than adults, are promised
   the forgiveness of sin through Christ's blood
   and the Holy Spirit who produces faith.
Therefore, by baptism, the mark of the covenant,
   infants should be received into the Christian church
   and should be distinguished from the children of unbelievers.
This was done in the Old Testament by circumcision,
   which was replaced in the New Testament by baptism.

Q & A 95 of the Westminster Shorter Catechism:

To whom is baptism to be administered?

Baptism is not to be administered to any that are out of the visible church, till they profess their faith in Christ, and obedience to him; but the infants of such as are members of the visible church are to be baptized.

WHAT ABOUT THE BIBLE?

Inerrancy has been so exalted as to become a chief characteristic of Scripture for many. Instead of placing emphasis on the saving truth of the Bible to bear witness to Christ, attention is focused rather on the precise accuracy of minor details. This unfortunate development does not do justice to the kind of book the Bible is. Minute inerrancy may be a central issue for the telephone book, but not for the psalms, proverbs, apocalyptic, and parables. Inerrancy just does not focus attention correctly where the Bible is concerned....It is alarming to consider how similar to the spirit and method of the Pharisees this preoccupation with the minutiae of the Bible is.

Clark Pinnock, "Three Views of the Bible in Contemporary Theology," *Biblical Authority,* p. 67

It is strange that the Bible is our most treasured book, and yet it seems so difficult that we don't find it very helpful. Perhaps we have expected the wrong things of it; we have asked of it what it cannot do. We have expected the Bible to keep promises that it has never made to us. The Bible cannot be a good luck piece to bring God's blessing. Nor can it be an answer book to solve our problems or to give us right belief.

Walter Brueggemann, *The Bible Makes Sense,* p. 9

Discussion of biblical authority is never a simple matter. There is a mystery surrounding the authority of the Bible which we can never completely fathom. The authority of the Bible is the authority of God himself and that can never be adequately defined but only confessed. We confess that the Bible is the inspired Word of God and that it is unconditionally authoritative for faith and life.

1971 Acts of Synod, Report 36, "The Nature and Extent of Biblical Authority," p. 465

In its view of biblical authority, liberal theology considers it important to insist that the Bible is merely a human text—written, copied, translated, and interpreted by fallible people. It contains all manner of internal contradictions, moral blemishes, legend and saga, inaccuracies and the like....To regard it as God's written Word is an idolatrous perversion of belief which must be dethroned.

Clark Pinnock, "Three Views of the Bible in Contemporary Theology," *Biblical Authority,* p. 51

When belief in the gospel opens one's eyes to the eternal God speaking through the Scriptures, those very words which to the unbelieving are simply religious literature (even sublime religious literature) are seen to be the infallible Word of the ever-living God. Such faith overleaps all inadequacies of human expression, all literary, cultural, numerical, geographical disparities, gaps, inconsistencies. Faith embraces the Word that speaks with the certainty, the assurance, the infallibility of God's covenant address to humankind.

Harry R. Boer, *Above the Battle?,* pp. 85ff.

Those whom the Holy Spirit has inwardly taught truly rest upon Scripture, and Scripture indeed is self-authenticated; hence, it is not right to subject it to proof or reasoning. And the certainty it deserves with us it attains by the testimony of the Spirit....Illumined by his power, we believe, neither by our own nor by anyone else's judgment, that Scripture is from God; but...we affirm with utter certainty...that it has flowed to us from the very mouth of God by the ministry of men. We seek no proofs, no marks of genuineness on which our judgment may lean; but we subject our judgment and wit to it as to a thing far beyond any guesswork.

John Calvin, *Institutes* I, vii, 5

The Word itself is not quite certain for us unless it be confirmed by the testimony of the Spirit....For the Lord has joined together the certainty of his

Word and of his Spirit so that the perfect religion of the Word may abide in our minds when the Spirit, who causes us to contemplate God's face, shines; and that we may in turn embrace the Spirit with no fear of being deceived when we recognize him in his own image, namely, in the Word.

John Calvin, *Institutes* I, ix, 3

Central Bible Institute
September 20

Dear Rev. Freed:

It's been four weeks since I arrived here at the Central Bible Institute. You were right about almost everything you said I could expect. Professor Kline was glad when I gave him greetings from you. From the way he responded, I think he was remembering some of the fun you had when you were in school together—but he didn't elaborate!

I haven't been very homesick—probably because I've been too busy to think of anything but my studies and the schedule we have to keep. Some of the rules are a bit rigid, but when I think about why I'm here, I tell myself it's worth some inconvenience. I'll adjust.

My real reason for writing you is that some of my old questions are coming back. It's ironic that I came to CBI to get some answers, and instead the questions keep coming back with greater force. I get disgusted with myself sometimes. Why can't I just believe? Why can't I just shut the questions off and trust? It's not that I'm not trusting the Lord. My problem is still with the Bible.

Remember that retreat we had last year? You spoke on "Why We Can Trust the Bible." You explained it so well that I thought my questions were answered once and for all. You said the Bible was the *inspired, infallible,* and *inerrant* Word of God, and that all three of those words are important in knowing why we can trust God's Word. Since the Holy Spirit inspired the Bible, there can be no mistakes in it. You explained that all the differences in the Gospels and all the apparent contradictions can be explained or could be harmonized if we had the original writings. Your important point was that if there was even one error in the Bible, we couldn't trust any of it. Isn't that what you said?

I want to believe that, and I *can* believe it as long as I'm listening to someone explain it at a retreat. But when I come home and read the Bible, all the questions come back. Sometimes I get the impression that the writers of the Bible didn't even *try* to be exact about all the details that look like inconsistencies. If Matthew, Mark, and Luke had *tried* to get all the details straight, we wouldn't even have to ask whether Jesus healed two blind men (Matt. 20:29–30) or one (Mark 10:45–47 and Matt. 18:35–38), or whether he did it when he was leaving Jericho (Matthew, Mark) or when he was coming to Jericho (Luke). I know it's a small thing. Personally, those differences wouldn't even bother me if it wasn't for our claim that if there's one mistake in the Bible we can't trust any of it. Our claim makes me notice those differences and feel like I have to resolve them.

That's where my problem lies. Our faith about the Bible shakes my faith in the Bible and gets in the way of my reading it. Rev. Freed, does our faith about the original writings apply to our copies and translations? I know you told us that we no longer have the original writings but that our present copies are, for all practical purposes, very reliable. Does the "not one mistake" teaching apply to the translations we use? And does it apply equally to all translations?

I hope you don't blame all this on Jack. It's true that I spend a lot of time with him, but please believe that these are my own questions. I love the Lord and I need the Bible, but our belief about why we can trust the Bible shakes my faith. Does that make sense?

It helps to write this down. Please be patient with me and take your time writing back. Tell Dad I really like it here at CBI.

Yours in Christ,
Kathy

Gethsemane Church
October 12

Dear Kathy:

Thanks for your letter. Yes, there is some irony in your problems with the Bible. Central Bible Institute is one of the great fortresses of the faith, one of the strongest defenders against modern rejection of the Bible. And you're wondering whether our translations of the Bible are the inerrant Word of God. Our belief that we can trust the Bible because it is free from all error is getting in your way of trusting and using it freely.

My first (and maybe best) advice is to ask your questions in class. Don't be afraid to do that. The professors and counselors will be ready to help you find good answers.

Have you heard of the book entitled *Battle for the Bible* by Harold Lindsell (Grand Rapids: Zondervan, 1976)? Professor Lindsell says, as I did at the retreat, that the Bible is the inspired, infallible, and inerrant Word of God. He even uses the last two words interchangably. He doesn't argue that, and I don't have to either— that's not your question. You ask whether our present copies of the Bible can be trusted in spite of errors that may have crept in through copying and translating. Lindsell answers:

97

Any student of lower criticism admits that there have been copyists' mistakes made by those who diligently sought to reproduce the books of the Bible by hand. But a copyist's mistake is something entirely different from an error in Scripture. A misspelled or a misplaced word is a far cry from error, by which is meant a misstatement or something that is contrary to fact.

In short, Kathy, I believe with Harold Lindsell that the original Scriptures are inerrant and that the present translations are inerrant for all practical purposes. Your Bible is the inerrant Word of God even though it may have copyists' or translators' mistakes in it.

Does that make sense to you? We must talk when you come home. God bless you in your studies.

Yours in Christ,
Pastor Freed

Central Bible Institute
October 29

Dear Rev. Freed:

Thanks for your letter. I've been asking my questions in class and I think it helps. But I had an experience last week that makes me wonder about many things.

A few friends and I have been attending Macedonia Baptist Church where most of the members are black. It was scary at first, but we wanted to see what other churches are like. What a welcome we received! Their kindness makes me embarrassed about what happened at our church last year when Jack brought one of his black friends to visit. Anyway, it was beautiful to be so welcomed and to feel the power of the music, the preaching, and the prayer. We liked it enough to accept their invitation to come to the Wednesday prayer meeting.

Last Wednesday we stayed afterwards to talk with the pastor and his assistant who teaches at the local high school. We were learning a lot about the church when I asked my question: "Do you believe the Bible is inerrant?" The pastor asked what I meant and I explained. He smiled a bit and said, "Well, sister, I haven't thought much about that, but I suppose so." That really bothered me.

What kind of answer is that: "I suppose so"? The assistant pastor sensed my problem and tried to explain that their church doesn't have a highly developed teaching about the Bible like many of our churches do. He was careful to explain it without offending us. He talked about the slave days when most slaves couldn't read, so they learned what the Bible said instead. They listened to the Bible stories and teachings and put many of them into songs.

He explained that their church has been so concerned about freedom and survival that they haven't wondered about my question. They are more concerned about "getting in touch with the power of the Bible," as he put it.

I'm troubled by all of that. I love to go there, but I can't handle all the questions I get when I'm there—like at the prayer meeting last Wednesday when the sister prayed for the passage of the school millage and a brother prayed that a certain person would get elected mayor. I couldn't believe they did that out loud. In our church we're so careful to keep political issues out of our prayers.

I still like CBI. Good classes and good friends. But I will need a long visit when I get home. Right now I feel like my questions are getting bigger and my answers smaller. How can that pastor say "I suppose so" when our whole faith depends on the inerrancy of the Bible?

Sincerely,
Kathy

Central Bible Institute
November 14

Dear Rev. Freed:
I haven't even given you a chance to re-spond to my last letter, but something has come up that I want you to know about. Can you stand some good news?

Professor Kline had us do some reading on the subject of understanding the Bible. Some of the readings were dull, but I found the subject itself quite interesting. Would you believe that I found some answers to my questions in a rather surprising way?

I did some reading about the scholars who are working all the time to find the most accurate reading of the Bible texts. It shook me at first to learn that there are about 4,500 Greek manuscripts of the New Testament alone and about 150,000 variations among them. But Professor Kline gave us examples of how he has been working on some of Paul's letters for the past five summers. It was exciting to learn how comparing the manuscripts and following certain guidelines leads us as close as possible to an accurate, original reading of the text. And it was downright reassuring to learn that not a single teaching of the Bible is in doubt in spite of all the variations!

One student asked Professor Kline if his faith depends on finding which text is the most accurate. He said, "Well, Martin Luther discovered the gospel in the most corrupt translation of the New Testament—the Latin Vulgate. I don't think he would have discovered it any sooner if he had a more accurate text. Does that answer your question?"

Now I'm working on another assignment called "backgrounds." We have to take a New Testament book (I chose Hebrews) and study its authorship, date, situation, style, and purpose. It's the kind of assignment I really like because it opens up the richness and uniqueness of each part of the Bible. One of the students admitted in class that he reads the Bible as though it had been written last year in Missouri and published in New York. I always knew there was a big difference between the Psalms and Galatians, but I never paid attention to how important that difference was in understanding the message.

I think I know now why I was having so much trouble at first. I was letting my belief about the Bible get in the way of the Bible itself. My theories were more important to me than the Bible! And when the pastors at Macedonia Baptist didn't immediately understand my question about the Bible, I couldn't understand how they could love the Lord the way they do. I'm almost ashamed to say that my belief about the Bible was keeping me from the Bible. I know you didn't teach me that, but that's what I was doing. Please know that the Bible is becoming more of an open book to me than it was before.

When we talk during the Christmas break, I'll need some help. The term paper for Kline's course is due at the end of January, and I want to work on it while I'm home. The topic I've chosen, and Kline has approved, is: "How our faith about the Bible affects how we use it." If you have any resources for me, please keep them ready.

Yours in the Lord,
Kathy

Gethsemane Church
December 2

Dear Kathy:

Welcome home—in advance. I could have waited to respond to your last letters until you arrived for the holiday and would have done so if it weren't for the candlelight service. Would you be willing to play your flute for the usual numbers? You may let me know when you get home.

I like your term paper topic and, yes, I do have some resources you may use.

Your experience at Macedonia Baptist reminded me of my grandmother—God rest her soul. When I was in the seminary, I asked her what she believed about the Bible. She looked puzzled and said, "I can't live without it. Is that what you mean?" That wasn't what I meant, but maybe it's what I should have meant. I tend to forget that some Christians have not been caught up in the questions that modern secularism has raised about the Bible. I sort of envy them.

But someone has to face the challenge of skepticism. That's really what I had in mind at that retreat last year. My main concern, Kathy, is that what we believe about the Bible is in keeping with and based upon the Bible itself. Your letter about how our beliefs can get in the way of faith made me think. Maybe I have overreacted to wrong views of the Bible.

See you soon, the Lord willing. And bring your flute!

Yours in Christ,
Pastor Freed

_____

What *do* we believe about the Bible? Are there mistakes in it? And does our whole faith depend on its inerrancy?

FOR FURTHER READING

Nederhood, Joel. *Promises, Promises, Promises.* Grand Rapids, Mich.: Board of Publications of the Christian Reformed Church, 1979.

> The personal, intimate reflections of a Reformed pastor and radio minister on the Scriptures. Chapter 26, "Theopneustos," addresses the question of the divine authority of the Bible.

Rogers, Jack, ed. *Biblical Authority.* Waco, Tex.: Word Books, 1977.

> A collection of essays by evangelicals who question the inerrancy doctrine, while affirming clearly the truth and trustworthiness of God's Word.

Van der Leeuw, Gerardus. *The Bible as a Book.* St. Catharines, Ont.: Paideia Press, 1978.

> A brief, simple, concise guide to reading the Bible as a book and hearing its proclamation as the Word of God.

SESSION GUIDE

CHALLENGE 7   WHAT ABOUT THE BIBLE?

A. Personal notes/questions on Challenge 7

February 19, 1985

How does the Bible set us free from the law of God?
Read the entire book of Romans - Next Tuesday!
do B+C. Summarize Romans 1-3, 3-8, 9-16,

B. Discussing Challenge 7

1. Describe the three approaches to the Bible that Kathy encountered: Rev. Freed's, Macedonia Baptist Church pastor's, and Professor Kline's. Which of those is closest to your own view of the Bible?

2. What other approaches to or views of the Bible have you encountered from Christian people?

3. Of the following two attitudes toward the Bible and its authority, which would you find most difficult to argue with? Why?

    a. I think we should admit that there are lots of mistakes in the Bible. After all it's written by human authors and all humans make mistakes. That doesn't take away from the fact that I can learn about God, Jesus Christ, and the Christian way from the Bible. It's still the book of my faith.

    b. I think we must accept the entire Bible, every word, as true and factual. To admit even one error would destroy the basis of my faith. There may be minor mistakes by people who copied the Bible, but nothing it says is in any way contrary to fact. If scientists say something different, they're wrong, not the Bible.

C. Developing a Reformed answer

1. From a Reformed perspective, what is the "key question" we should ask about the Bible?

2. Try to summarize in a sentence or two what you believe about the *authority* of the Bible. Use Challenge 7 and section *D* for reference.

3. On what does accepting the Bible as authoritative ultimately depend? How important is our faith in the authority of the Bible?

4. What practical suggestions do you have for helping the power and authority of God's Word to work in our lives?

D. Resources

Article III of the Belgic Confession

We confess that this Word of God was not sent nor delivered by the will of man, but that *men spake from God, being moved by the Holy Spirit,* as the apostle Peter says; and that afterwards God, from a special care which He has for us and our salvation, commanded His servants, the prophets and apostles, to commit His revealed word to writing....

Article V of the Belgic Confession

We receive all these books...as holy and canonical, for the regulation, foundation, and confirmation of our faith; believing without any doubt all the things contained in them, not so much because the Church receives and approves them as such, but more especially because the Holy Spirit witnesses in our hearts that they are from God....

Article VII, Chapter 1 of the Westminster Confession of Faith

The authority of the Holy Scripture, for which it ought to be believed, and obeyed, dependeth not upon the testimony of any man, or Church; but wholly upon God (who is truth itself) the author thereof: and therefore it is to be received, because it is the Word of God.

Article VII, Chapter 1 of the Westminster Confession

All things in Scripture are not alike plain in themselves, nor alike clear unto all: yet those things which are necessary to be known, believed, and observed for salvation, are so clearly propounded...that not only the learned, but the unlearned...may attain unto a sufficient understanding of them.

HOW SHOULD WE EVANGELIZE?

The ultimate motive of evangelism, then, must be love of God. It is *the* motive of evangelism, embracing and excelling all other worthy motives.

R. B. Kuiper, *God-Centered Evangelism,* p. 87

The salvation of souls, the growth of Christ's church, even the coming of Christ's kingdom, of momentous importance though they may be and actually are, are but means to a still higher end, the highest of all ends—God's glorification.

R. B. Kuiper, *God-Centered Evangelism,* p. 101

It is a matter of supreme importance to maintain that the Word of God is the one and only indispensable means by which the Holy Spirit works faith in the hearts of men. Although this does not mean that the Word always operates in isolation from every other conceivable factor, another factor never serves as a substitute for the Word. At most it is only auxiliary and subsidiary to the Word.

R. B. Kuiper, *God-Centered Evangelism,* p. 123

In the field of evangelism, pre-evangelism is everything that gets a person ready to hear the reconciling and redeeming Word. There are many lumps, rocks, and patches of hard soil that resist the seed of God's Word. A man may have to experience many things before he is personally ready to receive the Seed and profit from an evangelism encounter.

Charles S. Mueller, The Strategy of Evangelism, p. 66

When the Reformers selected the right preaching of the Word and the proper administration of the sacraments as the definitive marks of the church, they laid hold of two essentials of the Christian faith. Where their definitions are inadequate is in the decisive area of mission. Historically, these men were in no position to think of mission as we must think of it today. Hence, we must go beyond them. The times in which we live differ from the time in which they lived. Actually, in this regard, we are closer sociologically to the writers of the New Testament than we are to the Reformers, because we—like Paul, the writers of the Gospels, and others—must formulate what we believe not in contrast to what other Christians do, but by being in God's mission in God's world.

John H. Piet, The Road Ahead, p. 37

The message of the church is God's good news. But is it not also bad news? Does it not have a dark side, like the moon? What about sin and judgment and hell? Are these not bad news? And does the church not preach sin and judgment and hell?

The answer to all these questions is No. There is only one message that God has for man—the good news, the gospel.

Christians, Schipper, and Smedes, eds., Who in the World?, p. 24

The main feature of the biblical view of evangelism which we have been seeking to expound, in contrast to some modern evangelism, is its God-centeredness. . . . Let it be said that our greatest need in evangelism today is the humility to let God be God.

J. R. Stott, Our Guilty Silence, p. 113

Derek and Ellen Matthews awoke to the sight of a moving van parked in front of the house directly behind them. It must have arrived during the night. They had been watching for some activity there ever since the Shanks moved out six weeks earlier. Derek was not sorry to see them leave. Their parties were frequent and loud and had kept the children awake on more than one summer night.

In some ways Ellen was glad to see them leave, too, but she was left with an ache. She had prayed for them, brought their children to vacation Bible school and to the film series at the church, and had tried to learn how to love them. She felt she had failed.

Derek left for work. Ellen watched the house while she began her morning routine. If the truck was there, the new neighbors were sure to follow. Looking across the backyards, she remembered the day Elsie Shanks came running straight through the hedge, carrying the limp body of two-year-old Keith. His fall down the stairs had left him unconscious. All the way to the hospital Elsie had sobbed, "Oh, my God." When he recovered in the emergency room and was no worse for the experience, Elsie had apologized for her behavior. "I never could handle emergencies," she said.

There were those long talks over coffee in the morning. They talked about the children, the neighborhood, the schools, their pasts, and their opinions on safe subjects. Ellen talked about the church and about what the children had prayed when they went to bed. Sometimes she even ventured to say something about her faith in Christ. But whenever she came uncomfortably close, Elsie would pull back. "I'm just not religious," she'd explain quickly. "I'm not *against* religion, you understand, but I've never cared to get involved in it."

Ellen liked Elsie and cared deeply about her. She often thought it would be easier to know what to say and do if Elsie were hostile to the faith rather than merely distant. She prayed for her conversion and for wisdom and courage to say the right words. None of her approaches had pierced the simple defense: "I'm not religious." All the tools and techniques for witnessing that she had learned seemed to work best with people she didn't know. But she *knew* Ed and Elsie. Their carefree unbelief withered her witness and left her frustrated.

The doorbell rang. A short, bearded man with a slightly foreign look stood on the porch, looking as though he was lost.

"Hello. I'm Joe Hernandez, your new neighbor. Ed Shanks said to stop here if we needed help. Are you Ellen Matthews?"

"Yes. Come in. Welcome. Do you know Elsie and Ed?"

"Do I know Elsie and Ed?" he laughed. "Who doesn't? Ed and I worked together in Minneapolis. When he heard that I had a job here, he called and rented his house to us. That's why the sale sign is down. We've leased the house for six months, and if we like it, we'll buy it."

"Welcome to the neighborood. Is there something we can do? It must be a big day for you."

"I'd like to use the phone to call the utilities and the phone company. We hope to get moved in today."

They talked long enough to ease the edge of unfamiliarity and to assure each other of good will. When Joe was ready to leave, he noticed the small emblem of the fish on the front door.

"That makes me feel at home. We have good friends in Minneapolis who had the same sign on the door. They got it from the church. What does it mean again?"

"We're Christians," said Ellen.

"That's right, I remember now. Well, I'd better be getting back. Thanks for your help. You'll be seeing more of us, I'm afraid."

Ellen saw a lot of her new neighbors that day. She provided the small favors that made an unpleasant day tolerable for Joe and Helene Hernandez and their two children. By the time Derek came home from work, Ellen was full of news about the Hernandez family. Over dinner Ellen and Derek talked about the similarity in ages between their children and the Hernandez boys and discussed what they could do to help Joe and Helene feel welcome in the neighborhood. When they finished eating, they followed their custom of reading a paragraph from the Bible and praying. Ellen was arrested by the words of Jesus: "I am the way, and the truth, and the life; no one comes to the Father, but by me" (John 14:6). They prayed for their new neighbors—and for Ed and Elsie Shanks.

The words from John's Gospel were good preparation for the meeting at the church that evening. Ellen and Derek had signed up with five others to attend a six-week course on "Evangelism Methods" led by the pastor. When they arrived, Derek was glad to see that the seven members of the group knew each other well enough to dispense with the usual get-acquainted games. Some of the pastor's attempts to make everyone feel at home had the opposite effect on him. He had disliked it when the course in the Minor Prophets started out with a game in which everyone had to guess each other's favorite dessert. This time the reading of John 4 and prayer were enough to prepare for the subject at hand.

The pastor distributed an outline for the six sessions beginning with "Why We Are Here" (Session 1) and concluding with "Practice and Report" (Session 6). He began by asking each of the persons present to say why he or she had come to the class. He wanted to be sure that his purpose would fit their needs and expectations.

Dan Bechman didn't even raise his hand. He was there because he wanted to see results in evangelism. In his business, profits were the bottom line and salesmanship was the key to success. The same was true for the church, Dan insisted. Saving souls was the bottom line, and selling the gospel was the way to succeed. He was tired of the weekly routine of worship and work, and of the same songs and seasons year after year. He pointed out that only four adults were added through evangelism in the last year. "That adds up to only one convert for every thirty-five communicants—no business could survive that way," he said. He pressed his point by showing that if each Christian adult led one person to Christ in one year, the whole world would be converted in one generation. He wanted *results.*

Beverly Sims was next. She was there because she wasn't sure what evangelism really meant. She had been a counselor for the Billy Graham Crusade three years earlier and had followed up on three inquirers. Two were marginal Christians who revived their commitment to their churches. One was a troubled mother whose problems led her to a hospital, brought her to divorce, and required that she move out of town. Beverly couldn't reconcile her experiences as a counselor with her expectations of the crusade. She wanted to know what evangelism meant and how she could do it without having to wait for another crusade.

Derek was there, he said, because he and Ellen had agreed to take one adult education course at the church each year. "This is my last chance to keep my promise this year, so here I am," he said, nudging her playfully. He explained that he was fulfilled in his service to Christ, expected to enjoy the class, and hoped to learn something helpful. He had no specific questions that needed answers.

Ellen said she was there because she felt guilty. She wished she could be like Derek—confident in his faith and content with his limitations—but she felt she had to improve her witness. She had failed, she said, to evangelize Elsie and Ed Shanks (although Derek disagreed). Now she had new neighbors. She needed help in becoming a more

effective witness. For the sake of her own faith, as well as her neighbors, she didn't want to fail again.

Julie Evers had just enrolled as a student at Junior College. She was uncertain about her major and her future, but she was sure that Christ wanted her to be a witness for him. She was looking for some techniques that would help her be an evangelist at her new school. With so much uncertainty in her life, she wanted to be sure about her relationship to Christ.

Mae Miller was there, she confessed, not because she needed to learn about evangelism methods, but because she had something to share. She had found an evangelism tool that had changed her life and witness—and she was sure it could be the key to satisfying the longing in the church and the needs of the world. The tool was a small, folded card that could be used by any Christian anywhere and at anytime. It could be left as a tract, but it was more effective when it was used to initiate conversation. It was entitled "Three Spiritual Secrets," and it described, with diagrams, who we are without Christ, who we are with Christ, and who we can become with the Holy Spirit in us. The Secrets method had been field tested and was found to be 73 percent successful in airports, 61 percent successful at county fairs, and 47 percent successful on college campuses. It was a simple, direct method of evangelism that had revolutionized her life and could revive the church. She wanted it included in the course.

Dave Steiner was there, he said, because he loved his new church and wanted to learn all he could. He described it as a privilege to worship and serve Christ there. He was one of the four new members Dan had mentioned, and he was still exploring the faith that had brought new peace and purpose to his life. The adult Sunday school class had opened his eyes to how Christians can celebrate the joys and endure the tragedies of life. He had lived for pleasure and prosperity long enough, and it had cost him plenty. Now he wanted to read and learn all he could about the Christian faith and life to make up for lost time. If he could help others discover the satisfaction of knowing Christ and the church, that would be a bonus for him. But meanwhile, he had so much catching up to do that he would have to attend to his own needs as well.

When Dave finished, there was silence. The pastor sat there, looking around the circle. Everyone waited for him to say something reassuring, profound, or holy.

All he could say was "Wow!"

No one realized until then how much tension had built among them. It was a relief to laugh.

"I think we just changed our agenda," he said.

"What does that mean?" asked Dan.

"Well, we gathered to learn 'Evangelism Methods' as though we all agreed what evangelism is and why we do it. But among us we have many motives mixed in with our faith and love for Christ. It sounds like we need to understand from our Reformed perspective what evangelism's all about. We need a little evangelism right here while we prepare to evangelize others."

"Is that a problem?" asked Julie.

"No. It's our opportunity."

They talked freely and agreed that their own need for the gospel and for understanding evangelism was important in preparing to evangelize. The pastor promised to prepare a Bible study in evangelism for the next meeting. The assignment: read Acts 1 through 5.

When Derek and Ellen returned home, they found the tools they had loaned to Joe and Helene on the kitchen table. In a vase there was a single rose, and a note that read: "Thanks for being here. Joe and Helene."

How should Derek and Ellen evangelize their new neighbors?

FOR FURTHER READING

Bavinck, J. H. *An Introduction to the Science of Missions.* Philadelphia: The Presbyterian and Reformed Publishing Co., 1960.

Although aimed more at the foreign mission task, this book gives an excellent biblical study of "the foundation of missions" and a combined biblical and cultural analysis of "the missionary approach."

Biblical Evangelism. Grand Rapids, Mich.: Board of Home Missions, Christian Reformed Church, 1980.

A brief study of the principles of evangelism and how they should be applied in the local church.

Boer, Harry R. *Pentecost and Missions.* Grand Rapids, Mich.: Wm. B. Eerdmans Pub. Co., 1961.

A study of biblical thought on missions which roots our witnessing in Pentecost and the Spirit's power.

Green, Michael. *Evangelism in the Early Church.* Grand Rapids, Mich.: Wm. B. Eerdmans Pub. Co., 1970.

A superb historical study of how the Christian church of the first centuries evangelized.

Kuiper, R. B. *God-centered Evangelism.* Grand Rapids, Mich.: Baker Book House, 1961.

The presentation of a Reformed approach to evangelism.

SESSION GUIDE

CHALLENGE 8   HOW SHOULD WE EVANGELIZE?

A. Personal notes/questions on Challenge 8

B. Answering the challenge

   Meet with two other people and make a list of several specific suggestions for Derek and Ellen on how to evangelize their new neighbors. What, if anything, should they do?

C. Discovering the Reformed perspective

   Read through the scriptural and creedal references in section *E*. Skim the opening quotes in Challenge 8. Then attempt to draw up an accurate list of Reformed principles of evangelism.

   [handwritten notes]
   ①Love of God
   ①the growth of Christ's church.
   ②Bible is the most important way by which the Holy Spirit works ... ④Evangelism in steps. ⑤Gods mission in Gods world.
   ⑥Message of God is Good News
   ⑦God-centeredness

   Compare your list with the ideas written in Response 8.

D. Applying the Reformed perspective

   1. Review author Van Harn's suggestions for Derek and Ellen (end of Response 8). How do his ideas reflect a Reformed view of evangelism?

2. Review the ideas of the class for evangelizing the new neighbors (section *B*). Which ideas, if any, might we now want to question as possibly non-Reformed notions of evangelism? Are there any new ideas we might now add to the list?

3. Has this lesson—and *Reasons* in general—helped you understand when and how you should witness or defend your faith? Please comment.

E. Resources

"So everyone who acknowledges me before men, I also will acknowledge before my Father who is in heaven."   Matthew 10:32

"Go therefore and make disciples of all nations."   Matthew 28:19

"You shall receive power when the Holy Spirit has come upon you; and you shall be my witnesses...to the end of the earth."   Acts 1:8

And his gifts were that some should be...evangelists, some pastors and teachers, to equip the saints for the work of ministry, for building up the body of Christ.
Ephesians 4:11–12

Always be prepared to give an answer to everyone who asks you to give the reason for the hope that you have.   1 Peter 3:15 (NIV)

To be reconciled to God is to be sent into the world as his reconciling community....
Christ has called the church to this mission and given it the gift of the Holy Spirit.
Confession of 1967 II, A, 1

There must be ministers...to preach the Word of God and to administer the sacraments; also elders and deacons...that by these means the true religion may be preserved, and the true doctrine everywhere propagated.
Belgic Confession, Article XXX

Unto this catholic visible Church Christ hath given the ministry...for the gathering and perfecting of the saints...and doth, by His own presence and Spirit, according to His promise, make them effectual thereunto.
Westminster Confession of Faith, Chapter XXV, Article 3

Bibliography

Acts of Synod, 1971. Grand Rapids, Mich.: Board of Publications of the Christian Reformed Church, 1971.

Barton, Bruce. *The Man Nobody Knows.* Indianapolis: Bobbs-Merrill Co.; New York: Grosset & Dunlap, 1925.

Biéler, André. *The Politics of Hope.* Grand Rapids, Mich.: Wm. B. Eerdmans Pub. Co., 1974.

Boer, Harry R. *Above the Battle?* Grand Rapids, Mich.: Wm. B. Eerdmans Pub. Co., 1977.

Boersma, T. *Is the Bible a Jigsaw Puzzle?* St. Catharines, Ont.: Paideia Press, 1978.

Brand, Eugene L. *Baptism: A Pastoral Perspective.* Minneapolis, Minn.: Augsburg, 1975.

Brokering, Herbert. *I-Opener.* St. Louis: Concordia Publishing House, 1974.

Brueggemann, Walter. *The Bible Makes Sense.* Atlanta: John Knox Press, 1977.

Calvin, John. *Commentary on the Harmony of the Evangelists, Matthew, Mark and Luke.* Grand Rapids, Mich.: Wm. B. Eerdmans Pub. Co., 1949.

——————. *Commentary on the Pastoral Epistles.* Grand Rapids, Mich.: Wm. B. Eerdmans Pub. Co., 1948.

——————. *Institutes of the Christian Religion.* Edited by John T. McNeill. Translated by Ford Lewis Battles. Library of Christian Classics, vols. 1, 4. Philadelphia: Westminster Press, 1960.

Christians, Schipper, and Smedes, eds., *Who in the World?* Grand Rapids, Mich.: Wm. B. Eerdmans Pub. Co., 1972.

Daane, James. *The Freedom of God.* Grand Rapids, Mich.: Wm. B. Eerdmans Pub. Co., 1973.

De Vos, Richard. *Believe!* Old Tappan, N.J.: Fleming H. Revell Co., 1975.

De Vries, Peter. *The Mackerel Plaza.* New York: Signet Books, 1959.

Fackre, Gabriel. *The Christian Story.* Grand Rapids, Mich.: Wm. B. Eerdmans Pub. Co., 1978.

Hammarskjold, Dag. *Markings.* New York: Alfred A. Knopf Inc., 1965.

Hoekema, Anthony A. *The Bible and the Future.* Grand Rapids, Mich.: Wm. B. Eerdmans Pub. Co., 1979.

Kahn, Herman and Kurtz, Paul. *Images of the Future.* Edited by Robert Bundy. Buffalo: Prometheus, 1976.

Kreeft, Peter. "Toward Uniting the Church" *The Reformed Journal,* January 1979, pp. 10–14.

Kuiper, R. B. *God-Centered Evangelism.* Grand Rapids, Mich.: Baker Book House, 1961.

Kuyvenhoven, Andrew. "The Late Great Planet Earth." *The Banner,* March 17, 1972, pp. 4–6.

Lewis, C. S. *Mere Christianity.* London: Geoffrey Bles, 1952.

Lindsell, Harold. *Battle for the Bible.* Grand Rapids, Mich.: Zondervan Publishing House, 1976.

Lindsey, Hal. *The Late Great Planet Earth.* Grand Rapids, Mich.: Zondervan Publishing House, 1970.

Maccoby, Hyam. *Revolution in Judea.* London: Orbach and Chambers, 1973.

Marty, Martin E. *Baptism.* Philadelphia: Fortress Press, 1962.

Mead, Frank S. *Handbook of Denominations in the United States.* New 6th ed. Nashville: Abingdon, 1975.

Mouw, Richard. *Politics and the Biblical Drama.* Grand Rapids, Mich.: Wm. B. Eerdmans Pub. Co., 1976.

Mueller, Charles S. *The Strategy of Evangelism.* St. Louis, Mo.: Concordia Publishing House, 1965.

Niebuhr, H. Richard. *Christ and Culture.* New York: Harper & Row, 1951.

Piet, John H. *The Road Ahead.* Grand Rapids, Mich.: Wm. B. Eerdmans Pub. Co., 1970.

Plantinga, Cornelius, Jr. *Beyond Doubt*. Grand Rapids, Mich.: Board of Publications of the Christian Reformed Church, 1980.

—————. *A Place to Stand*. Grand Rapids, Mich.: Board of Publications of the Christian Reformed Church, 1980.

Rogers, Jack, ed. *Biblical Authority*. Waco, Tex.: Word Inc., 1977.

Schweitzer, Albert. *The Quest of the Historical Jews*. 3d ed. London: George Allen & Unwin Ltd., 1954.

Scofield, C. I., ed. *The New Scofield Reference Bible*. New York: Oxford University Press, 1967.

Scott, J. R. *Our Guilty Silence*. Grand Rapids, Mich.: Wm. B. Eerdmans Pub. Co., 1967.

Spurgeon, Charles Haddon. *The Early Years Autobiography*. Edinburgh, London: Banner of Truth, 1967.

Stearn, Jess. *Edgar Cayce—The Sleeping Prophet*. New York: Doubleday Pub. Co., 1967.

Stringfellow, William. *An Ethic for Christians and Other Aliens in a Strange Land*. Waco, Tex.: Word Inc., 1973.

Thibodeaux, Mary Roger, S. B. S. "A Black Nun Looks at Black Power." *Mission Trends No. 4: Liberation Theologies*. New York: Paulist Press; Grand Rapids, Mich.: Wm. B. Eerdmans Pub. Co., 1979.

Toffler, Alvin, ed. *The Futurists*. New York: Random House, 1972.

"Vetoes Church Baptism." *The Christian Century,* June 3–10, 1981, p. 633.

White, Bouck. *The Call of the Carpenter*. Garden City, N.Y.: Doubleday Pub. Co., 1911.